BLACKTOWN LIBRARY

b12800899d

P9-DYJ-881

BOOK SALE

# Pressure Cookers

Published in 2010 by Murdoch Books Pty Limited

Murdoch Books Pty Ltd
Pier 8/9
23 Hickson Road,
Millers Point NSW 2000
Phone: + 61 (0) 2 8220 2000
Fax: + 61 (0) 2 8220 2558
www.murdochbooks.com.au

Murdoch Books UK Limited
Erico House, 6th Floor
93–99 Upper Richmond Road
Putney, London SW15 2TG
Phone: +44 (0)20 8785 5995
Fax: +44 (0)20 8785 5985
www.murdochbooks.co.uk

Publisher: Kay Scarlett
Design concept and illustrations: Heather Menzies
Designer: Katy Wall
Food Editor: Anneka Manning
Editor: Kim Rowney
Production: Joan Beal
Recipes developed by Brett Sargent, Alison Adams, Peta Dent, Michelle Earl, Vicky Harris and the
Murdoch Books Test Kitchen Team

National Library of Australia Cataloguing-in-Publication Data
Title: Pressure Cookers. Includes index.
ISBN 9781741968941 (pbk.)
Subjects: Pressure cookery.
Dewey number: 641.587

© Text Murdoch Books Pty Limited 2010. All rights reserved.
© Design and illustrations Murdoch Books Pty Limited 2010. All rights reserved.
No part of this publication may be reproduced, stored in a retrieval system or transmitted in any form or by any means, electronic,
mechanical, photocopying, recording or otherwise, without the prior written permission of the publisher.

PRINTED IN CHINA

# Pressure Cookers

### more than 100 easy recipes

MURDOCH BOOKS

**Blacktown City Library**

| Supp. | date. | PR. | LCN |
|---|---|---|---|
| DON | 12·1·11 | $19·50 | 361033. |
| 641.587 PRES | | | 2/11 |
| SHG | b12800899d | | |

# Contents

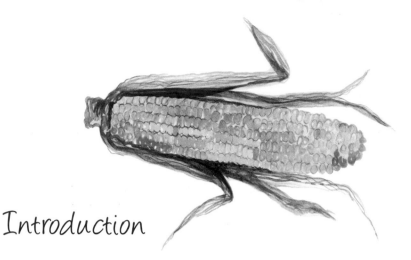

# Introduction

The very first version of the pressure cooker, known as a 'Steam Digester', was invented by Denis Papin, a French physicist, back in 1679. Early models were very cumbersome and extremely dangerous to use because it was difficult to regulate the steam and control the temperature.

It wasn't until 1939 that the first commercially produced modern saucepan-style pressure cookers became available. They featured an easy-to-close interlocking cover, and soon manufacturers were finding it hard to keep up with the demand for them due to their revolutionary time-saving advantages. Since then, the pressure cooker industry has continued to develop and improve the many styles and features available to the home cook.

Even though pressure cookers have always enjoyed a popularity in Europe and Asia, they have experienced a resurgence in recent times in countries such as Australia and the United States. And the reasons are good ones:

- They are a great time saver — dishes that traditionally take hours to cook can be prepared in a pressure cooker in a fraction of the time, some up to 70 per cent faster.

- Pressure cookers are cost-saving — cheaper cuts of meat are most suited to pressure cooking making it an economical way to cook.

- Nutritionally they get a tick — the shorter cooking time means that generally more nutrients are retained, as well as flavour.

- Pressure cookers are great energy savers — because of the shorter cooking time, less energy is needed in the cooking process (a big benefit for today's world).

# How a pressure cooker works

Different models of pressure cookers can look quite different, and have different valves, regulators and locking systems, but they all work in a similar way.

Food is cooked using the pressure that is created by the steam trapped in it. Pressure cookers have a lid that can, when locked in place, completely seal the pot. When the liquid in the pot boils and creates steam, the steam is trapped in the pot, building up and increasing the pressure and, in turn, increasing the boiling point of the liquid as well as the temperature within the cooker.

The pressure of the trapped steam is measured in psi (or pound of force per square inch). Check your owner's manual for the cooking pressure of your cooker. Some pressure cookers have both low and high settings. Generally 'low' will mean a psi of around 8, while 'high' will mean a psi of 12 to 15. A psi of 15 is the highest pressure a modern-day cooker will reach.

The higher the psi the higher the pressure and temperature in the cooker and the faster the food will cook. All our recipes specify either a 'low' or 'high' pressure setting when cooking. The pressure cookers used for testing the recipes in this book had a psi of 8 when set on low, and a psi of 13 when set on high.

In the past, pressure cookers have had a slightly infamous reputation for not being completely safe to use. Disasters involving the lid being forced off during cooking due to excess pressure building up, resulting in the contents of the pot being sprayed around the kitchen, are well known by many.

Thankfully, modern pressure cookers are much safer. They have a number of safety features, including safety mechanisms that prevent the lid being removed before the pressure is completely released. They also have valves that will automatically release the pressure if it becomes too high.

# Buying a pressure cooker

When it comes to size, pressure cookers generally range from around 4 litres (140 fl oz) to 10 litres (350 fl oz). A 4 litre (140 fl oz) cooker is ideal for singles or couples and smaller meals. The 6 litre (210 fl oz) cooker is a great size for most dishes serving 4–6 people. However, if you plan on braising lots of large cuts of meat or if you have a large family, consider an 8 litre (280 fl oz) or 10 litre (350 fl oz) one.

Consider the cooking pressure levels of the pressure cooker — some only have one psi level while others offer at least two. More than one pressure level will give you greater control and flexibility when cooking various foods.

When choosing a pressure cooker consider that the most durable are made of stainless steel with a 3-ply aluminium 'sandwich' base. Those with a heavy 'sandwich' base are good for browning meats before you add the liquid, they cook more evenly and will be less likely to scorch and develop 'hot spots'. It is also a good idea to choose a pressure cooker with heat-resistant handles.

Steaming baskets are a good pressure cooker accessory and many are sold with them. They are useful when steaming vegetables and cooking dishes such as meatloaf (see page 79) that needs to be elevated above the water or sauce.

And remember, you get what you pay for as far as pressure control and ease of use goes.

# Using your pressure cooker

Always read your owner's manual carefully before you use your pressure cooker for the first time and follow all the recommendations.

As with all cooking appliances, you will have to get to know your pressure cooker — for example, how quickly it cooks and how much liquid it needs. Note the results of the recipes you cook so you can adjust the cooking time and/or liquid content the next time if necessary.

In our recipes we have specified the size of the pressure cooker used. If using a different sized cooker, you may need to alter the cooking time slightly.

## Ingredients

Liquid is probably the most important ingredient when pressure cooking. As a general rule, your pressure cooker will need at least 250 ml (9 fl oz /1 cup) liquid for the first 15 minutes of cooking and an additional 150 ml (5 fl oz) for every extra 15 minutes (or part thereof) of cooking time. This is what all our recipes have been based on. However, pressure cookers do vary slightly and it is best to check the instruction manual to see if the manufacturer recommends a different amount.

More liquid can be added to these recipes, but never less — just make sure you don't fill the pot more than two-thirds full of combined food and liquid. If adding more liquid, just remember that the final consistency of the dish will be slightly wetter.

Never fill your pressure cooker more than two-thirds full with combined food and liquid. However, if you are cooking ingredients that absorb liquid and expand during cooking (for example, grains such as rice and pearl barley, or pulses such as chickpeas, dried beans, lentils and dried split peas), don't fill your cooker more than half full.

Never use 'creamy' liquids such as milk, cream, coconut milk or coconut cream as the only liquid in the dish. Either water or stock also needs to be added to dilute these ingredients, to reduce the risk of scorching during cooking.

Small amounts of yoghurt are fine to add to dishes before cooking under pressure, such as in a marinade, but generally yoghurt is best stirred through the dish at the end of cooking once the pressure has been released.

There are a few things that don't cook well in a pressure cooker. These include pasta, dumplings and porridge. Dishes with flour also don't work well as they tend to scorch more easily. If using flour, only use it in small quantities, such as for dusting meats before browning them.

Generally, it's a good idea to initially seal meats in a little oil until well browned before adding the liquid ingredients, as this helps develop a good flavour. Similarly, vegetables used as a flavour-base, such as onions, leeks and celery, and herbs and spices are often best cooked in a little oil for a short whle first for the same reason.

Always prick foods with skins, such as sausages, before cooking. Cut the same ingredients into similar-sized pieces so they will cook at the same rate.

## Bringing the cooker up to pressure

If you have seared meat or other ingredients in the cooker, make sure you scrape up any bits clinging to the base of the pot. Adding a little wine, stock or water and simmering this for a short time while scraping the pot will help dislodge them. This will help prevent food scorching on the base of the cooker while pressure-cooking.

Always check the gasket or rubber seal and the valves in the lid. The gasket should be flexible, not damaged and have no food sticking to it. These things can prevent the lid from sealing correctly. The valves should also be free of food, which can prevent them from working properly and steam not being regulated or released properly. Your manual will have further instructions about what to look for and correct maintenance for the gasket and valves.

Make sure your lid is correctly positioned and locked before you bring the cooker up to pressure. Your pressure cooker should be over a heat source that covers about one-third of the base of the pot. Use this heat source on high to bring the cooker to the desired pressure.

If using an electric stovetop, once the desired pressure is reached over high heat, transfer the pressure cooker immediately to a similar-sized burner set to low. This way the pressure can be stabilised immediately without waiting for the electric burner to reduce to low.

If using a gas stovetop, never let the flames come up around the side of the pot as it may damage it.

It can take as little as 1 minute or as long as 15 minutes for a cooker to come up to pressure, depending on the pressure cooker itself, what you are cooking and how much liquid the dish contains. Our 'cooking time' at the beginning of our recipes doesn't include bringing the cooker up to pressure or depressuring it due to this variation in time.

## Maintaining the pressure

Once the pressure is reached, as registered by the valve or regulator on the lid, turn down the heat to the lowest possible setting to stabilise the pressure. There should only be a gentle hissing coming from the valve, if any at all. If it is more forceful, reduce the heat even further to reduce the steam being released and to stabilise it.

Always use a timer — timing is crucial when using a pressure cooker. Start timing as soon as the specified pressure is reached. This is easy to tell with those models that have inbuilt timers as they will be activated automatically. For those that don't, start timing from the moment that there is a constant and stable jet of steam being released through the valve and once you have stabilised the pressure.

Keep an eye on the pressure and stove heat at all times, as they need to be kept consistent and well regulated for the best results.

Be prepared to adjust the heat if needed during cooking. After the first few uses of your pressure cooker you will quickly work out which burner on your stovetop is most suitable.

A heat diffuser is a great accessory to have on hand when getting to know your pressure cooker. If your cooker doesn't have a heavy bottom, or you have an unpredictable heat source or one that isn't low enough to stabilise the pressure, the food may scorch on the base of the cooker. A heat diffuser, when placed between the heat and the cooker, will spread the heat evenly over the bottom of the pot and reduce the intensity of the heat, helping to prevent scorching. It is also very helpful to use when cooking rice, grains and pulses to prevent these from sticking and scorching.

You may have to play around with it a little to get the heat level correct while using the diffuser, but once you've worked it out the results will be great.

# Releasing the pressure

There are two ways of releasing the steam and, in turn, pressure from your cooker — the 'natural' and automatic or 'quick' release methods. The recipes in this book will specify which one to use.

● Natural release method — To release the pressure naturally, simply remove the cooker from the heat and set it aside until the pressure is released. Generally this method is recommended for dishes such as curries, casseroles, stews and braises using cheaper cuts of meats as well as larger, whole cuts of meat, as they will often toughen if the pressure is released too quickly. This method is also recommended for beans and potatoes as it helps them hold onto their skins.

● Automatic or 'quick' release method — Some pressure cookers have an automatic 'quick' release method. Check your manual and, if it does, simply follow the instructions. If it doesn't, you can still release the steam, and therefore the pressure, quickly by running cold water over the top of the cooker away from vents and the regulator until all the pressure is released — it won't take long. This method is good to use when adding extra ingredients during the cooking process or for those foods that easily overcook such as fish and vegetables.

You may need to add different ingredients at different times during cooking depending on the time they take to cook. If so, release the pressure using the 'quick' release method, stir in the additional ingredients, lock the lid back in place and then continue with the recipe. It is well worth doing to make the most of the flavour and texture of individual ingredients.

## Finishing a dish

When removing the lid from the cooker once the pressure has been released, lift it up facing away from you, to protect you from any escaping steam that may burn.

If you feel your dish has too much liquid at the end of the cooking time (different pressure cookers will often affect the remaining liquid content in a dish) you can thicken the sauce by simmering it, uncovered, in the pot until the desired consistency and flavour is achieved. Alternatively, you can blend a little plain (all-purpose) flour or cornflour (cornstarch) with a little of the cooking liquid before returning it to the pot, and then simmer it for a few minutes while stirring.

## Cleaning and storing your pressure cooker

Always read and follow the care instructions for your pressure cooker.

Wash the gasket separately by hand in warm soapy water. The lid shouldn't be immersed in water as the safety valves can be damaged. The pot is best washed by hand and dried immediately, although some can be put into the dishwasher — check your manual for specific recommendations.

Store your cooker with the lid off. Never lock it in place, as the gasket can be damaged and any odours will be trapped inside. If the lid is locked in place and there is any moisture trapped inside, it will be near impossible to remove the lid.

# Cooking rice in a pressure cooker

Put the unrinsed rice and water or stock into a 6 litre (210 fl oz) pressure cooker. Lock the lid in place and bring to the specified pressure over high heat. Once the pressure is reached, reduce the heat to stabilise the pressure and cook for the specified time. Release the pressure and then carefully remove the lid. Stir the rice with a fork to separate the grains. Lock the lid back in place and stand for 5 minutes before serving.

*Note* *All times are based on 8 psi for 'low' pressure and 13 psi for 'high' pressure.*

| Rice | Quantity | Water or stock quantity | Pressure level | Cooking time | Release method |
|------|----------|-------------------------|----------------|--------------|----------------|
| White medium–grain | 200 g (7 oz/1 cup) | 350 ml (12 fl oz) | Low | 7 minutes | natural |
| White long-grain | 200 g (7 oz/1 cup) | 350 ml (12 fl oz) | Low | 6 minutes | natural |
| Jasmine | 200 g (7 oz/1 cup) | 350 ml (12 fl oz) | Low | 6 minutes | natural |
| Basmati | 200 g (7 oz/1 cup) | 350 ml (12 fl oz) | Low | 6 minutes | natural |
| Brown long-grain | 200 g (7 oz/1 cup) | 500 ml (17 fl oz/2 cups) | Low | 23 minutes | natural |
| Brown medium–grain | 200 g (7 oz/1 cup) | 375ml (13 fl oz/ 1½ cups) | Low | 17 minutes | natural |

# Cooking dried pulses in a pressure cooker

Rinse the pulses. If needed, soak the pulses in plenty of water for at least 8 hours or overnight. Drain well. Put the drained pulses and specified quantity of water or stock into a 6 litre (210 fl oz) pressure cooker. Lock the lid in place and bring to the specified pressure over high heat. Once pressure is reached, reduce the heat to stabilise the pressure and cook for the specified time. Release the pressure and then carefully remove the lid. Drain the pulses of any residual liquid.

*Note All times are based on 8 psi for 'low' pressure and 13 psi for 'high' pressure.*

| Pulse | Quantity | Soak overnight | Water or stock quantity | Pressure level | Cooking time | Release method |
|-------|----------|----------------|-------------------------|----------------|--------------|----------------|
| Red kidney beans | 210 g (7½ oz/1 cup) | yes | 750 ml (26 fl oz/3 cups) | High | 20 minutes | natural |
| Cannellini beans | 200 g (7 oz/1 cup) | yes | 750 ml (26 fl oz/3 cups) | High | 8 minutes | natural |
| Black-eyed peas | 200 g (7 oz/1 cup) | yes | 750 ml (26 fl oz/3 cups) | High | 8 minutes | natural |
| Chickpeas | 220 g (7¾ oz/1 cup) | yes | 750 ml (26 fl oz/3 cups) | High | 10 minutes | natural |
| Pearl barley | 200 g (7 oz/1 cup) | yes | 1 litre (35 fl oz/4 cups) | High | 15 minutes | natural |
| Puy lentils | 200 g (7 oz/1 cup) | no | 1 litre (35 fl oz/4 cups) | Low | 18 minutes | natural |
| Green/brown lentils | 185 g (6½ oz/1 cup) | no | 500 ml (17 fl oz/2 cups) | Low | 12 minutes | natural |

# Vegetables

Vegetables cook very quickly in the pressure cooker, retaining their garden fresh colour and all their nutrients.

# BUTTERNUT PUMPKIN SOUP

preparation time: 15 minutes
cooking time: 20 minutes
serves: 4

20 g (3/4 oz) butter
1 onion, chopped
1 carrot, chopped
2 teaspoons ground cumin
1 teaspoon freshly grated nutmeg
1.25 kg (2 lb 12 oz) butternut
    pumpkin (squash), peeled, seeded
    and chopped into even-sized chunks

1 all-purpose potato, peeled and
    chopped
750 ml (26 fl oz/3 cups) vegetable
    or chicken stock
60 ml (2 fl oz/1/4 cup) pouring cream
1 tablespoon chopped flat-leaf
    (Italian) parsley, to garnish

- Melt the butter in a 6 litre (210 fl oz) pressure cooker over medium heat and cook the onion and carrot for 10 minutes or until the onion softens. Add the cumin and nutmeg and cook for a further 2 minutes or until aromatic.

- Add the pumpkin, potato and stock to the cooker, season with salt and freshly ground black pepper and stir well. Lock the lid in place and bring the cooker to high pressure over high heat. Once high pressure is reached, reduce the heat to stabilise the pressure and cook for 5 minutes or until the pumpkin is tender.

- Remove the cooker from the heat and release the pressure using the natural release method. Remove the lid carefully. Allow the mixture to cool slightly.

- Using a hand-held stick blender, purée the mixture until smooth. Alternatively, transfer the soup mixture to a food processor and purée until smooth.

- Ladle the soup into bowls and serve drizzled with cream and sprinkled with parsley.

*Vegetables*

# FRENCH ONION SOUP

**preparation time:** 15 minutes
**cooking time:** 20–25 minutes
**serves:** 4

40 g (1<sup>1</sup>/<sub>2</sub> oz) butter
1 tablespoon olive oil
1 kg (2 lb 4 oz) brown onions,
   thinly sliced
250 ml (9 fl oz/1 cup) dry white wine

2 tablespoons brandy (optional)
750 ml (26 fl oz/3 cups) beef stock
4 thyme sprigs
2 tablespoons finely chopped flat-leaf
   (Italian) parsley, to garnish

• Heat the butter and oil in a 6 litre (210 fl oz) pressure cooker over medium–high heat and cook the onion for 10–15 minutes or until golden (don't brown too much or the soup will become bitter).

• Stir in the wine, brandy (if using), stock, 250 ml (9 fl oz/1 cup) water and the thyme. Lock the lid in place and bring the cooker to high pressure over high heat. Once high pressure is reached, reduce the heat to stabilise the pressure and cook for 10 minutes.

• Remove the cooker from the heat and release the pressure using the natural release method. Remove the lid carefully.

• Season to taste with salt and freshly ground black pepper. Sprinkle with the parsley and serve with crusty bread.

*Vegetables*

# CAULIFLOWER AND ALMOND SOUP

**preparation time:** 15 minutes
**cooking time:** 20 minutes
**serves:** 4

20 g (3/4 oz) butter
2 teaspoons olive oil
1 large leek, white part only, chopped
2 garlic cloves, crushed
1 kg (2 lb 4 oz) cauliflower, cut into
   small florets
2 (about 375 g/13 oz) all-purpose
   potatoes, peeled and diced

1.5 litres (52 fl oz/6 cups) vegetable
   or chicken stock
75 g (2 1/2 oz/1/2 cup) blanched
   almonds, chopped
1/3 cup snipped chives
pouring cream, to serve

• Heat the butter and oil in a 6 litre (210 fl oz) pressure cooker over medium heat and cook the leek for 10 minutes or until softened. Add the garlic and cook for a further 2 minutes or until aromatic.

• Add the cauliflower, potato and stock to the cooker and stir well. Lock the lid in place and bring the cooker to high pressure over high heat. Once high pressure is reached, reduce the heat to stabilise the pressure and cook for 5 minutes or until the cauliflower and potato are very tender.

• Remove the cooker from the heat and release the pressure using the natural release method. Remove the lid carefully. Allow the mixture to cool slightly.

• Using a hand-held stick blender, purée the mixture with the almonds. Alternatively, transfer the soup mixture and almonds to a food processor and purée until smooth. Stir through half the chives and season with salt and freshly ground black pepper. Ladle the soup into bowls, drizzle with a little cream and garnish with the remaining chives.

*Note* The soup will thicken on standing. Stir through extra stock if needed.

*Vegetables*

# POTATO AND LEEK SOUP

**preparation time:** 15 minutes
**cooking time:** 20 minutes
**serves:** 4

2 teaspoons olive oil
20 g ( 3/4 oz) butter
2 leeks, white part only, thinly sliced
2 celery stalks, chopped
1 carrot, chopped
2 prosciutto slices, roughly chopped

4 all-purpose potatoes, peeled and
   roughly chopped
500 ml (17 fl oz/2 cups) vegetable
   or chicken stock
pouring cream, to serve

- Heat the oil and butter in a 6 litre (210 fl oz) pressure cooker over medium heat and cook the leek, celery, carrot and prosciutto for 10 minutes or until the leek softens.

- Add the potato, stock and 500 ml (17 fl oz/2 cups) water to the cooker and stir well. Lock the lid in place and bring the cooker to high pressure over high heat. Once high pressure is reached, reduce the heat to stabilise the pressure and cook for 8 minutes.

- Remove the cooker from the heat and release the pressure using the natural release method. Remove the lid carefully. Allow the mixture to cool slightly.

- Using a hand-held stick blender, purée the mixture until smooth. Alternatively, transfer the soup mixture to a food processor and purée until smooth.

- Season to taste with salt and freshly ground black pepper. Ladle the soup into bowls and serve drizzled with a little cream.

*Vegetables*

# TOMATO, SPINACH AND RISONI SOUP

preparation time: 15 minutes
cooking time: 25 minutes
serves: 4

1 tablespoon olive oil
1 onion, finely chopped
1 leek, white part only, thinly sliced
1 garlic clove, crushed
1/2 teaspoon ground cumin
750 ml (26 fl oz/3 cups) chicken or
vegetable stock

500 g (1 lb 2 oz/2 cups) tomato
passata (puréed tomatoes)
200 g (7 oz) smoked ham, chopped
200 g (7 oz/1 cup) risoni (see Note)
250 g (9 oz) English spinach,
trimmed and leaves shredded
1 1/2 tablespoons lemon juice

- Heat the oil in a 6 litre (210 fl oz) pressure cooker over medium heat and cook the onion and leek for 10 minutes or until softened. Add the garlic and cumin and cook for a further 2 minutes or until aromatic.

- Add the stock, 500 ml (17 fl oz/2 cups) water, tomato passata and ham to the cooker and stir well. Lock the lid in place and bring the cooker to high pressure over high heat. Once high pressure is reached, reduce the heat to stabilise the pressure and cook for 10 minutes. Remove the cooker from the heat and release the pressure using the natural release method. Remove the lid carefully.

- Meanwhile, cook the risoni in a large saucepan of boiling water, following the packet directions, until al dente. Drain and rinse briefly.

- Add the spinach to the cooker and simmer for 1–2 minutes or until just wilted. Stir through the risoni and lemon juice. Season to taste with salt and freshly ground black pepper and serve with crusty bread.

*Note* Risoni looks like rice but is actually a type of pasta, often used in soups and stews. If unavailable, use any type of small soup pasta.

*Vegetables*

# CREAM OF MUSHROOM SOUP

**preparation time:** 15 minutes (+ 20 minutes soaking)
**cooking time:** 30 minutes
**serves:** 4

10 g ($1/4$ oz) dried porcini mushrooms
20 g ($3/4$ oz) butter
1 leek, white part only, thinly sliced
1 tablespoon olive oil
100 g ($31/2$ oz) pancetta or bacon, chopped
200 g (7 oz) Swiss brown mushrooms, roughly chopped

300 g ($101/2$ oz) mushroom flats, roughly chopped
80 ml ($21/2$ fl oz/$1/3$ cup) Madeira (Malmsey) (see Note)
500 ml (17 fl oz/2 cups) vegetable or chicken stock
2 teaspoons chopped marjoram
150 ml (5 fl oz) pouring cream
marjoram leaves, extra, to garnish

• Soak the porcini in 250 ml (9 fl oz/1 cup) boiling water for 20 minutes. Drain, reserving the soaking water.

• Melt the butter in a 6 litre (210 fl oz) pressure cooker over medium heat and cook the leek for 10 minutes or until softened. Remove from the cooker and set aside.

• Heat half the oil in the cooker over medium–high heat and cook the pancetta for 5 minutes or until crisp. Add to the leek. Add the remaining oil and Swiss brown mushrooms to the cooker and cook over medium–high heat for 3–5 minutes or until starting to soften.

• Add the porcini and the reserved soaking water to the cooker with the leek and pancetta mixture, mushroom flats, Madeira, stock, 250 ml (9 fl oz/1 cup) water and half of the chopped marjoram. Stir well. Lock the lid in place and bring the cooker to high pressure over high heat. Once high pressure is reached, reduce the heat to stabilise the pressure and cook for 10 minutes.

*Vegetables*

- Remove the cooker from the heat and release the pressure using the natural release method. Remove the lid carefully. Allow the mixture to cool slightly.

- Using a hand-held stick blender, purée the mixture. Alternatively, transfer the soup mixture to a food processor and purée until smooth, then return the soup to the pressure cooker.

- Stir through the cream and reheat over medium heat, uncovered, without boiling. Stir through the remaining chopped marjoram. Garnish with marjoram leaves and serve with crusty bread.

*Note Madeira is a fortified wine made in Portugal. Malmsey is the richest and fruitiest of the Madeiras and it can also be drunk as an after-dinner drink. If unavailable, use sherry.*

# VEGETABLE AND CHEDDAR SOUP

preparation time: 10 minutes
cooking time: 5 minutes
serves: 4

2 all-purpose potatoes (about
   250 g/9 oz), peeled and diced
2 zucchini (courgettes), diced
1 carrot, diced
1 celery stalk, diced
3 spring onions (scallions), finely
   chopped

1 litre (35 fl oz/4 cups) vegetable or
   chicken stock
1 x 400 g (14 oz) tin creamed corn
125 g (4$^{1}/_{2}$ oz/1 cup) grated
   cheddar cheese
2 tablespoons finely chopped flat-leaf
   (Italian) parsley

- Put the potato, zucchini, carrot, celery and spring onion in a 6 litre (210 fl oz) pressure cooker. Stir in the stock and season well with salt and freshly ground black pepper.

▶

▶ • Lock the lid in place and bring the cooker to high pressure over high heat. Once high pressure is reached, reduce the heat to stabilise the pressure and cook for 5 minutes.

• Remove the cooker from the heat and release the pressure using the natural release method. Remove the lid carefully.

• Stir in the creamed corn, half the cheese and the parsley. Season with salt and freshly ground black pepper. Serve immediately, sprinkled with the remaining cheese.

*Note If preferred, you can add some barbecued shredded chicken or chopped ham at the end of cooking, adding it at the same time as the corn and cheese.*

## MINESTRONE

**preparation time:** 15 minutes
**cooking time:** 25 minutes
**serves:** 6–8

1 tablespoon olive oil
1 onion, finely chopped
1 celery stalk, diced
100 g (3$^1$/$_2$ oz) pancetta or bacon, diced
2 garlic cloves, crushed
1 carrot, diced
2 all-purpose potatoes, peeled and cut into 1 cm ($^1$/$_2$ inch) dice
750 ml (26 fl oz/3 cups) chicken or vegetable stock
500 g (1 lb 2 oz/2 cups) tomato passata (puréed tomatoes)

100 g (3$^1$/$_2$ oz) ditalini or macaroni pasta
100 g (3$^1$/$_2$ oz) green beans, cut into 2 cm ($^3$/$_4$ inch) pieces
100 g (3$^1$/$_2$ oz) English spinach leaves, shredded
1 x 400 g (14 oz) tin cannellini beans, drained and rinsed (see Note)
1 small handful basil, torn
1 small handful flat-leaf (Italian) parsley, roughly chopped
freshly grated parmesan cheese, to serve

• Heat the oil in a 6 litre (210 fl oz) pressure cooker over medium heat and cook the onion, celery and pancetta for 10 minutes or until the onion softens. Add the garlic and cook for a further 2 minutes or until aromatic.

• Add the carrot, potato, stock, 250 ml (9 fl oz/1 cup) water and the tomato passata to the cooker and stir well. Lock the lid in place and bring the cooker to high pressure over high heat. Once high pressure is reached, reduce the heat to stabilise the pressure and cook for 8 minutes.

• Meanwhile, cook the pasta in a large saucepan of salted boiling water, following the packet directions, until al dente. Drain and rinse briefly.

• Remove the cooker from the heat and release the pressure using the natural release method. Remove the lid carefully.

• Add the green beans to the pressure cooker and simmer, uncovered, for 3 minutes. Stir in the drained pasta, spinach and cannellini beans. Simmer for a further 1–2 minutes or until the beans are just tender and the spinach has wilted.

• Stir through the basil and parsley and season to taste with salt and freshly ground black pepper. Ladle the soup into bowls and sprinkle with the parmesan. Serve with crusty bread.

*Note* *You can replace the tinned cannellini beans with 240 g (8$^1$/2 oz/1$^1$/3 cups) cooked dried cannellini beans (see page 15 for pressure cooking instructions).*

# RIBOLLITA

**preparation time:** 15 minutes
**cooking time:** 20 minutes
**serves:** 4–6

1 x 400 g (14 oz) tin chopped
   tomatoes
2 x 400 g (14 oz) tins cannellini
   beans, drained and rinsed
   (see Notes)
2 tablespoons extra virgin olive oil
1 carrot, diced
1 celery stalk, thinly sliced diagonally
1 bacon slice, finely chopped
1 garlic clove, crushed
$1/2$ teaspoon dried oregano
$1/4$ cabbage, thinly shredded

300 g ($10^1/2$ oz) all-purpose
   potatoes, peeled, cut into 1 cm
   ($1/2$ inch) dice
1 litre (35 fl oz/4 cups) vegetable or
   chicken stock
2 tablespoons tomato paste
   (concentrated purée)
100 g ($3^1/2$ oz) 'pane di casa' or
   crusty bread, broken into small
   chunks
50 g ($1^3/4$ oz/$1/2$ cup) freshly grated
   parmesan cheese
2 tablespoons shredded basil

● Place the tomatoes and half the cannellini beans in the bowl of a food processor. Process until puréed.

● Heat the olive oil in a 6 litre (210 fl oz) pressure cooker over medium heat and cook the carrot, celery and bacon for 5 minutes. Add the garlic and oregano and cook for a further 2 minutes or until aromatic.

● Add the tomato–bean purée, cabbage, potato, stock and tomato paste to the cooker and stir well. Season with freshly ground black pepper. Bring to a simmer over high heat and stir well again. Lock the lid in place and bring the cooker to high pressure over high heat. Once high pressure is reached, reduce the heat to stabilise the pressure and cook for 8 minutes or until the potato is tender.

• Remove the cooker from the heat and release the pressure using the natural release method. Remove the lid carefully.

• Stir the remaining cannellini beans, bread chunks and parmesan into the soup. Cook over medium heat, uncovered, for 1-2 minutes or until the cheese is melted and the soup is heated through. Taste and adjust the seasoning if necessary. Stir through the basil and serve.

*Notes You can replace the tinned cannellini beans with 480 g (8¹/2 oz/1 ¹/3 cups) cooked dried cannellini beans (see page 15 for pressure cooking instructions).*
*Ribollita literally means 'reboiled' and is a traditional Tuscan soup, often made in large quantities and reheated again the next day.*

# YELLOW CURRY WITH VEGETABLES

preparation time: 15 minutes
cooking time: 10 minutes
serves: 4

140 g (5 oz) cauliflower
2 long, thin eggplants (aubergines)
1 large red capsicum (pepper)
2 zucchini (courgettes)
200 g (7 oz) green beans
2 tablespoons yellow curry paste
1 tablespoon vegetable oil
1 x 400 ml (14 fl oz) tin coconut
   cream

125 ml (4 fl oz/¹/2 cup) vegetable
   stock
1¹/2 tablespoons fish sauce
2 teaspoons grated palm sugar
   (jaggery) or soft brown sugar
150 g (5¹/2 oz) baby corn
1 small red chilli, seeded and
   chopped, to garnish
coriander (cilantro) leaves, to garnish
lemon wedges, to serve

►

► • Prepare the vegetables. Cut the cauliflower into florets. Cut the eggplants, capsicum and zucchini into 1 cm (¹/2 inch) slices. Cut the beans into 3 cm (1¹/4 inch) lengths.

• Put the curry paste in a 6 litre (210 fl oz) pressure cooker and cook over medium heat for 2–3 minutes or until aromatic, adding 1 teaspoon of the oil if necessary. Stir in the coconut cream, stock, fish sauce and palm sugar and bring to a gentle boil. Add the prepared vegetables and corn and stir well.

• Lock the lid in place and bring the cooker to low pressure over high heat. Once low pressure is reached, reduce the heat to stabilise the pressure and cook for 2 minutes or until the vegetables are just tender.

• Remove the cooker from the heat and release the pressure using the quick release method. Remove the lid carefully.

• Taste and adjust the seasoning if necessary. Garnish the curry with the chilli and coriander, and serve with lemon wedges and steamed rice.

# CHICKPEA AND VEGETABLE CURRY

preparation time: 15 minutes
cooking time: 20 minutes
serves: 4–6

1 tablespoon olive oil
1 red onion, cut into thin wedges
2 tablespoons Indian curry paste
3 garlic cloves, crushed
1 red or green chilli, seeded, chopped
1 teaspoon ground cumin
$1/2$ teaspoon ground turmeric
1 x 400 g (14 oz) tin chopped tomatoes
125 ml (4 fl oz/$1/2$ cup) vegetable stock or water
1 x 185 ml (6 fl oz) tin coconut cream
1 large carrot, sliced diagonally into 3 cm ($1^1/4$ inch) chunks

250 g (9 oz) orange sweet potato, sliced diagonally into 3 cm ($1^1/4$ inch) chunks
250 g (9 oz) cauliflower, cut into florets
250 g (9 oz) broccoli, cut into florets
2 long, thin eggplants (aubergines) (about 100 g/$3^1/2$ oz in total), cut into 3 cm ($1^1/4$ inch) thick slices
1 x 400 g (14 oz) tin chickpeas, drained and rinsed (see Note)
155 g ($5^1/2$ oz/1 cup) fresh or frozen peas
1 small handful coriander (cilantro) leaves, to garnish

*Vegetables*

• Heat the oil in a 6 litre (210 fl oz) pressure cooker over medium heat and cook the onion for 5 minutes or until starting to soften. Add the curry paste, garlic, chilli, cumin and turmeric and cook for a further 2 minutes or until aromatic.

• Add the tomatoes, stock, coconut cream, carrot and orange sweet potato to the cooker and bring to a simmer over high heat. Lock the lid in place and bring the cooker to low pressure over high heat. Once low pressure is reached, reduce the heat to stabilise the pressure and cook for 2 minutes.

▶

▶ ● Remove the cooker from the heat and release the pressure using the quick release method. Remove the lid carefully. Stir in the cauliflower, broccoli and eggplant. Replace the lid immediately and lock in place. Bring the cooker back to low pressure over high heat. Once low pressure is reached, reduce the heat to stabilise the pressure and cook for 2 minutes.

● Remove the cooker from the heat and release the pressure using the quick release method. Remove the lid carefully.

● Add the chickpeas and peas to the cooker Cook, uncovered, over medium heat for 3 minutes or until the peas are just tender. Ladle the curry into large bowls and sprinkle with the coriander. Serve with rice.

*Note  You can replace the tinned chickpeas with 250 g (9 oz/1 1/2 cups) cooked dried chickpeas (see page 15 for pressure cooking instructions).*

*Vegetables*

# CALDO VERDE

preparation time: 10 minutes
cooking time: 30 minutes
serves: 4

1 tablespoon olive oil
1 chorizo sausage (about 185 g/
  6¹/₂ oz), diced
1 red onion, chopped
1.5 kg (3 lb 5 oz) all-purpose
  potatoes, peeled and chopped
2 garlic cloves, crushed

¹/₂ teaspoon smoked paprika
750 ml (26 fl oz/3 cups) vegetable
  stock
200 g (7 oz) silverbeet (Swiss chard)
  or kale, finely shredded
olive oil, to serve

● Heat the oil in a 6 litre (210 fl oz) pressure cooker over high heat and cook the chorizo for 5 minutes or until starting to brown. Remove from the cooker and set aside. Add the onion and cook over medium heat for 5 minutes or until the onion starts to soften. Add the potato and cook for a further 5 minutes. Add the garlic and paprika and cook for a further 2 minutes or until aromatic.

● Add the stock and 750 ml (26 fl oz/3 cups) water to the cooker and stir well. Lock the lid in place and bring the cooker to high pressure over high heat. Once high pressure is reached, reduce the heat to stabilise the pressure and cook for 8 minutes or until the potato is tender.

● Remove the cooker from the heat and release the pressure using the natural release method. Remove the lid carefully. Allow the mixture to cool slightly.

● Using a hand-held stick blender, purée until smooth. Alternatively, transfer the soup mixture to a food processor and blend until smooth. Return the soup to the cooker and stir in the chorizo and silverbeet. Cook over high heat, uncovered, until the silverbeet just wilts. Season to taste with salt and freshly ground black pepper and serve drizzled with a little olive oil.

*Vegetables*

31

# Chicken

Impress with this collection of recipes
for succulent chicken, cooked with ease
in your pressure cooker.

# CREAMY CHICKEN AND CORN SOUP

preparation time: 15 minutes
cooking time: 20 minutes
serves: 4–6

4 corn cobs
2 teaspoons olive oil
10 g ( 1/4 oz) butter
1 leek, white part only, chopped
1 large celery stalk, chopped
2 garlic cloves, chopped
1 bay leaf
1/2 teaspoon dried thyme

500 g (1 lb 2 oz) boneless, skinless
    chicken thighs, trimmed
1 litre (35 fl oz/4 cups) chicken stock
60 ml (2 fl oz/1/4 cup) sherry
1 large floury potato, such as russet,
    peeled cut into 1 cm (1/2 inch) dice
185 ml (6 fl oz/3/4 cup) pouring cream
snipped chives, to garnish

● Using a large knife, remove the corn kernels from the cobs.

● Heat the oil and butter in a 6 litre (210 fl oz) pressure cooker over medium heat and cook the leek and celery for 10 minutes or until softened. Add the garlic, bay leaf and thyme and cook for 1 minute or until aromatic.

● Add the corn, chicken, stock, sherry and potato to the cooker. Lock the lid in place and bring the cooker to high pressure over high heat. Once high pressure is reached, reduce the heat to stabilise the pressure and cook for 7 minutes or until the chicken is tender. Remove the cooker from the heat and release the pressure using the natural release method. Remove the lid carefully. Allow the mixture to cool slightly.

● Using kitchen tongs, remove the chicken to a board and allow to cool slightly. Discard the bay leaf. Purée the soup using a hand-held stick blender. When the chicken is cool enough to handle, shred the chicken and return the meat to the cooker. Add the cream and cook over low heat, uncovered, until just heated through. Serve sprinkled with the chives.

# THAI CHICKEN AND GALANGAL SOUP

**preparation time:** 15 minutes
**cooking time:** 10 minutes
**serves:** 4

500 g (1 lb 2 oz) boneless, skinless
   chicken breasts
700 ml (24 fl oz) tinned coconut milk
300 ml (10$^1$/$_2$ fl oz) chicken stock
2 x 5 cm ($^3$/$_4$ x 2 inch) piece galangal,
   thinly sliced
4 kaffir lime leaves, torn
1 tablespoon finely chopped, well
   rinsed coriander (cilantro) root

1–2 teaspoons finely chopped
   red chilli
2 tablespoons fish sauce
1$^1$/$_2$ tablespoons lime juice
3 teaspoons grated palm sugar
   (jaggery) or soft brown sugar
coriander (cilantro) leaves,
   to garnish

*Chicken*

● Put the chicken, coconut milk, stock, galangal, half the lime leaves, coriander root and chilli in a 6 litre (210 fl oz) pressure cooker. Season with salt and freshly ground black pepper. Lock the lid in place and bring the cooker to high pressure over high heat. Once high pressure is reached, reduce the heat to stabilise the pressure and cook for 5 minutes or until the chicken is tender.

● Remove the cooker from the heat and release the pressure using the natural release method. Remove the lid carefully.

● Using kitchen tongs, remove the chicken to a board and allow to cool slightly. When the chicken is cool enough to handle, shred the chicken. Return the chicken to the cooker with the fish sauce, lime juice, palm sugar and remaining lime leaves. Heat over low heat, uncovered, until warmed through.

● Ladle the soup into serving bowls and garnish with the coriander leaves.

# CHICKEN LAKSA

**preparation time:** 30 minutes
**cooking time:** 5 minutes
**serves:** 4

200 g (7 oz) dried rice vermicelli
   noodles
500 g (1 lb 2 oz) minced (ground)
   chicken
1 small red chilli, finely chopped
2 garlic cloves, finely chopped
1/2 small red onion, finely chopped
1 lemon grass stem, white part only,
   finely chopped
2 tablespoons chopped coriander
   (cilantro) leaves

95 g (3¹/4 oz/¹/3 cup) laksa paste
500 ml (17 fl oz/2 cups) chicken stock
2 x 400 ml (14 fl oz) tins coconut
   cream
8 fried tofu puffs, halved diagonally
90 g (3¹/4 oz/1 cup) bean sprouts
2 tablespoons shredded Vietnamese
   mint
1 small handful coriander (cilantro)
   leaves
lime wedges, to serve

• Put the vermicelli in a heatproof bowl, cover with boiling water and soak for
10 minutes, or until soft. Drain well. Meanwhile, to make the chicken balls, put the
chicken, chilli, garlic, onion, lemon grass and chopped coriander in a food processor.
Season with salt and ground white pepper and process until just combined. Roll
tablespoons of the mixture into balls with wet hands. Set aside.

• Put the chicken balls, laksa paste, stock and coconut milk in a 6 litre (210 fl oz)
pressure cooker. Lock the lid in place and bring the cooker to low pressure over high
heat. Once low pressure is reached, reduce the heat to stabilise the pressure and cook
for 4 minutes or until the chicken balls are cooked through. Remove the cooker from the
heat and release the pressure using the natural release method. Remove the lid carefully.

• Divide the vermicelli, tofu puffs and bean sprouts among four serving bowls and
ladle the soup over the top, dividing the chicken balls evenly. Garnish with mint and
coriander and serve with the lime wedges.

*Chicken*

# CANJA

preparation time: 15 minutes
cooking time: 10 minutes
serves: 6

3 ripe tomatoes
1 tablespoon olive oil
1 onion, cut into thin wedges
1 celery stalk, finely chopped
2.5 litres (87 fl oz/10 cups) chicken
    stock

2 x 250 g (9 oz) boneless, skinless
    chicken breasts
200 g (7 oz/1 cup) long-grain rice
1 teaspoon finely grated lemon zest
1 mint sprig
2 tablespoons lemon juice
2 tablespoons shredded mint

• Score a cross in the base of each tomato. Put the tomatoes in a heatproof bowl and cover with boiling water. Leave for 30 seconds, then transfer to cold water, drain and peel the skin away from the cross. Cut the tomatoes in half, scoop out the seeds and discard them, and chop the flesh.

• Heat the oil in a 6 litre (210 fl oz) pressure cooker over medium heat and cook the onion and celery for 5 minutes or until starting to soften. Add the chopped tomatoes, stock, chicken, rice, lemon zest and mint sprig to the pressure cooker. Lock the lid in place and bring the cooker to high pressure over high heat. Once high pressure is reached, reduce the heat to stabilise the pressure and cook for 5 minutes or until the chicken and rice are tender.

• Remove the cooker from the heat and release the pressure using the natural release method. Remove the lid carefully.

• Using kitchen tongs, tranfer the chicken to a board and cut into slices. Return to the cooker with the lemon juice and stir. Season to taste with salt and freshly ground black pepper. Stir in the mint just before serving.

_Chicken_

# CURRIED CHICKEN NOODLE SOUP

**preparation time:** 20 minutes
**cooking time:** 10 minutes
**serves:** 6

120 g (4¼ oz) dried rice vermicelli noodles

300 g (10½ oz) baby bok choy (pak choy)

1 tablespoon peanut oil

1 small red chilli, seeded and finely chopped

1 tablespoon finely chopped fresh ginger

2 tablespoons Indian curry powder

750 ml (26 fl oz/3 cups) good-quality chicken stock

2 x 400 ml (14 fl oz) tins coconut milk

2 x 200 g (7 oz) boneless, skinless chicken breasts

⅓ cup torn basil

lemon wedges, to serve

• Put the vermicelli in a heatproof bowl, cover with boiling water and soak for 10 minutes, or until soft. Drain well. Separate the bok choy leaves and slice the large leaves in half lengthways. Set aside.

• Meanwhile, heat the oil in a 6 litre (210 fl oz) pressure cooker over medium heat and cook the chilli, ginger and curry powder for 2 minutes or until aromatic. Stir in the stock and half the coconut milk, then add the chicken. Lock the lid in place and bring the cooker to low pressure over high heat. Once low pressure is reached, reduce the heat to stabilise the pressure and cook for 4 minutes or until the chicken is just cooked. Remove the cooker from the heat and release the pressure using the natural release method. Remove the lid carefully.

• Using kitchen tongs, transfer the chicken to a board and allow to cool slightly. When the chicken is cool enough to handle, shred the chicken. Add the bok choy and remaining coconut milk to the cooker. Bring to a simmer over high heat and then cook gently, uncovered, for 2–3 minutes or until the bok choy wilts. Stir through the chicken and basil. Divide the vermicelli among serving bowls and ladle the soup over.

*Chicken*

# BROWN RICE AND BARLEY RISOTTO WITH CHICKEN AND BARLEY

**preparation time:** 20 minutes (+ 6 hours soaking)
**cooking time:** 30 minutes
**serves:** 4

110 g (3³/₄ oz/¹/₂ cup) pearl barley
4 boneless, skinless chicken thighs
1 tablespoon olive oil
1 red onion, finely chopped
15 sage leaves, plus extra, to serve
330 g (11¹/₂ oz/1¹/₂ cups) medium-grain brown rice
600 g (1 lb 5 oz) pumpkin (winter squash), peeled, seeded and cut into 1 cm (¹/₂ inch) dice

560 ml (19¹/₄ fl oz/2¹/₄ cups) chicken stock
60 ml (2 fl oz/¹/₄ cup) white wine
150 g (5¹/₂ oz/1 cup) fresh or frozen peas
50 g (1³/₄ oz/¹/₂ cup) freshly grated parmesan cheese, plus extra, to serve

• Put the barley in a large bowl, cover with plenty of water and soak for 6 hours or overnight. Drain.

• Trim the chicken of excess fat and cut into bite-sized pieces. Heat the oil in a 6 litre (210 fl oz) pressure cooker over medium heat and cook the onion for 5 minutes or until softened. Add the sage and cook for 1 minute or until aromatic. Stir in the drained barley and 500 ml (17 fl oz/2 cups) water. Lock the lid in place and bring the cooker to high pressure over high heat. Once high pressure is reached, reduce the heat to stabilise the pressure and cook for 8 minutes.

• Remove the cooker from the heat and release the pressure using the quick release method. Remove the lid carefully.

• Stir the chicken, rice, pumpkin, stock and wine into the cooker. Season well with salt and freshly ground black pepper. Replace the lid immediately and lock in place. Bring the cooker back to high pressure over high heat. Once high pressure is reached, reduce the heat to stabilise the pressure and cook for 12 minutes or until the barley and rice are cooked. Remove the cooker from the heat and release the pressure using the natural release method. Remove the lid carefully.

● Mash the pumpkin with a fork and thoroughly mix the pumpkin through the rice until it looks 'creamy'. Stir in the peas and parmesan, cover and stand for 3 minutes or until the peas are cooked through.

● Season to taste with salt and freshly ground black pepper. Spoon into serving bowls and top with extra grated parmesan cheese and sage leaves.

# CREAMY TOMATO AND CHICKEN STEW

preparation time: 15 minutes
cooking time: 45 minutes
serves: 4

*Chicken*

1.5 kg (3 lb 5 oz) chicken pieces
2 tablespoons olive oil
300 g (10½ oz) small button mushrooms, halved
4 bacon slices, fat removed, roughly chopped
2 onions, chopped
1 garlic clove, crushed

1 x 400 g (14 oz) tin chopped tomatoes
250 ml (9 fl oz/1 cup) chicken stock
125 ml (4 fl oz/½ cup) pouring cream
2 tablespoons chopped flat-leaf (Italian) parsley
2 tablespoons lemon thyme

▶

▶ • Trim the chicken pieces of excess fat. Heat half the oil in a 6 litre (210 fl oz) pressure cooker over medium–high heat and cook the chicken in batches until well browned. Remove from the cooker and set aside.

• Heat the remaining oil in the cooker over medium–high heat and cook the mushrooms for 5 minutes or until tender. Remove and set aside. Add the bacon and onion and cook over medium heat for 10 minutes or until the onion is soft. Add the garlic and cook for 1 minute or until aromatic.

• Return the chicken to the cooker with the tomatoes and stock and bring to the boil over high heat. Stir well. Lock the lid in place and bring the cooker to high pressure over high heat. Once high pressure is reached, reduce the temperature to stabilise the pressure and cook for 8 minutes. Remove the cooker from the heat and release the pressure using the quick release method. Remove the lid carefully.

• Stir through the mushrooms and cream and simmer, uncovered, until the sauce has thickened slightly. Stir through the parsley and lemon thyme. Serve with mashed potatoes and green beans if desired.

# APRICOT CHICKEN

**preparation time:** 10 minutes (+ overnight marinating)
**cooking time:** 10 minutes
**serves:** 4

1 garlic clove, crushed
1 tablespoon grated fresh ginger
1 tablespoon ground coriander
1 tablespoon ground cumin
1 teaspoon ground cinnamon
2 tablespoons vegetable oil
4 x 280 g (10 oz) boneless, skinless

chicken breasts
400 ml (14 fl oz) tinned apricot nectar
1 tablespoon honey
1 tablespoon lemon juice
60 g (2$^{1}$/$_{4}$ oz/$^{1}$/$_{2}$ cup) slivered
    almonds, toasted
1 handful coriander (cilantro) leaves

- Combine the garlic, ginger, ground coriander, cumin, cinnamon and oil in a medium bowl. Add the chicken and toss well to coat. Cover and refrigerate overnight.

- Put the chicken and marinade into a 6 litre (210 fl oz) pressure cooker with the apricot nectar, honey and lemon juice. Bring to the boil over high heat. Lock the lid in place and bring the cooker to high pressure over high heat. Once high pressure is reached, reduce the heat to stabilise the pressure and cook for 5 minutes or until the chicken is tender.

- Remove the cooker from the heat and release the pressure using the quick release method. Remove the lid carefully.

- Season to taste with salt and freshly ground black pepper. Sprinkle with the toasted almonds and the coriander leaves and serve with rice.

# CHICKEN CASSEROLE WITH MUSTARD AND TARRAGON

preparation time: 15 minutes
cooking time: 25 minutes
serves: 4–6

30 g (1 oz) butter
1 onion, finely chopped
1 leek, white part only, thinly sliced
1 kg (2 lb 4 oz) boneless, skinless
  chicken thighs
1/2 teaspoon dried tarragon
1 garlic clove, finely chopped

125 ml (4 fl oz/1/2 cup) chicken stock
350 g (12 oz) button mushrooms,
  sliced
100 ml (31/2 fl oz) pouring cream
2 tablespoons dijon mustard
11/2 tablespoons lemon juice

▶

► • Melt the butter in a 6 litre (210 fl oz) pressure cooker over medium heat and cook the onion and leek for 10 minutes or until softened but not coloured.

• Trim the chicken of any fat, then cut into quarters. Add the chicken, tarragon, garlic and stock to the cooker and bring to the boil over high heat. Lock the lid in place and bring the cooker to high pressure over high heat. Once high pressure is reached, reduce the heat to stabilise the pressure and cook for 3 minutes. Remove the cooker from the heat and release the pressure using the quick release method.

• Add the mushrooms, cream and mustard and stir to combine. Replace the lid immediately and lock in place. Bring the cooker back to high pressure over high heat. Once high heat is reached, reduce the heat to stabilise the pressure and cook for a further 2 minutes.

• Remove the cooker from the heat and release the pressure using the quick release method. Remove the lid carefully. Bring back to the boil over high heat. Secure the lid again and cook over high heat for 2 minutes. Release the pressure using the quick release method. Remove the lid carefully.

• Simmer, uncovered, for 5–10 minutes or until the sauce has reduced to the desired consistency. Stir through the lemon juice. Serve with mashed potatoes and zucchini or green beans.

*Chicken*

# CHICKEN AGRODOLCE

preparation time: 15 minutes
cooking time: 25–30 minutes
serves: 6

1 tablespoon olive oil
1.2 kg (2 lb 10 oz) chicken pieces,
 skin removed
250 ml (9 fl oz/1 cup) chicken stock
125 ml (4 fl oz/1/2 cup) red wine
 vinegar
125 ml (4 fl oz/1/2 cup) dry white wine
1 garlic clove
1 tablespoon dried oregano

2 bay leaves
55 g (2 oz/1/4 cup firmly packed) soft
 brown sugar
220 g (73/4 oz/1 cup) pitted prunes
2 tablespoons capers, rinsed
175 g (6 oz/1 cup) green olives
1 handful flat-leaf (Italian) parsley,
 chopped

● Heat the oil in a 6 litre (210 fl oz) pressure cooker over medium–high heat and cook the chicken in batches until well browned.

● Return all the chicken to the cooker with the stock, vinegar, wine, garlic, oregano and bay leaves. Bring to the boil over high heat. Lock the lid in place and bring the cooker to high pressure over high heat. Once high pressure is reached, reduce the heat to stabilise the pressure and cook for 8 minutes.

● Remove the cooker from the heat and release the pressure using the natural release method. Remove the lid carefully.

● Stir in the sugar, prunes, capers and olives. Simmer, uncovered, for 5–8 minutes or until the sauce has reduced slightly and the prunes have started to collapse. Season with salt and freshly ground black pepper and stir through the parsley. Serve with mashed potato.

*Chicken*

# CHICKEN WITH CELERIAC AND MARJORAM

**preparation time:** 15 minutes
**cooking time:** 35 minutes
**serves:** 6

1 kg (2 lb 4 oz) boneless, skinless
   chicken thighs
1 tablespoon olive oil
1 leek, white part only, sliced
1 large celeriac, trimmed, peeled
   and diced

1 garlic clove, crushed
250 ml (9 fl oz/1 cup) chicken stock
200 ml (7 fl oz) pouring cream
2 small marjoram sprigs
1 handful flat-leaf (Italian) parsley,
   chopped

- Trim the chicken of any fat, then cut each thigh into quarters. Heat the oil in a 6 litre (210 fl oz) pressure cooker over medium–high heat and cook the chicken in batches until well browned. Remove from the cooker and set aside.

- Add the leek to the cooker and cook over medium heat for 5 minutes or until starting to soften. Add the celeriac and garlic and cook for a further 2 minutes or until aromatic.

- Return the chicken to the cooker with the stock, half the cream and the marjoram. Bring to the boil over high heat. Lock the lid in place and bring the cooker to high pressure over high heat. Once high pressure is reached, reduce the heat to stabilise the pressure and cook for 5 minutes or until the chicken is tender.

- Remove the cooker from the heat and release the pressure using the natural release method. Remove the lid carefully.

- Stir through the remaining cream and simmer, uncovered, for 5 minutes or until the sauce has reduced slightly. Season to taste with salt and freshly ground black pepper. Stir through the parsley and serve with steamed asparagus if desired.

*Chicken*

# COQ AU VIN

preparation time: 20 minutes
cooking time: 40 minutes
serves: 4

1.5 kg (3 lb 5 oz) chicken (see Note)
1 tablespoon olive oil
250 g (9 oz) bacon, diced
20 baby onions, peeled
375 ml (13 fl oz/1¹/₂ cups) red wine
375 ml (13 fl oz/1¹/₂ cups) chicken
    stock
125 ml (4 fl oz/¹/₂ cup) brandy

2 teaspoons tomato paste
    (concentrated purée)
2 bay leaves
2 thyme sprigs
250 g (9 oz) small button mushrooms
60 g (2¹/₄ oz) butter, softened
40 g (1¹/₂ oz/¹/₄ cup) plain
    (all-purpose) flour

• Joint the chicken into eight pieces by removing both legs and cutting between the joint of the drumstick and the thigh. Cut down either side of the backbone and lift it out. Turn the chicken over and cut through the cartilage down the centre of the breastbone. Cut each breast in half, leaving the wing attached to the top half.

• Heat the oil in a 6 litre (210 fl oz) pressure cooker over medium–high heat and cook the chicken in batches until well browned. Remove and set aside.

• Add the bacon and onions to the cooker and cook over medium–high heat for 5 minutes or until lightly golden. Add the wine and simmer for 2 minutes, scraping the base of the pot. Return the chicken to the cooker with the stock, brandy, tomato paste, bay leaves and thyme. Bring to the boil over high heat. Lock the lid in place and bring the cooker to high pressure over high heat. Once high pressure is reached, reduce the heat to stabilise the pressure and cook for 8 minutes.

• Remove the cooker from the heat and release the pressure using the quick release method. Remove the lid carefully.

▶

Chicken

▶ • Add the mushrooms, replace the lid immediately and lock in place. Bring the cooker back to high pressure over high heat. Once high pressure is reached, reduce the heat to stabilise the pressure and cook for a further 3 minutes or until the chicken and mushrooms are tender. Remove the cooker from the heat again and release the pressure using the natural release method. Remove the lid carefully.

• Lift out the chicken and vegetables with a slotted spoon and place them on a plate, then cover and set aside.

• Mix together the butter and flour and whisk into the sauce in the cooker. Cook over medium heat, stirring, until thickened and simmering, then return the chicken and vegetables to the sauce to heat through. Serve with steamed potatoes.

*note* *Alternatively, buy 1.5 kg (3 lb 5 oz) chicken pieces.*

## CHICKEN AND PRUNE TAGINE

**preparation time:** 15 minutes
**cooking time:** 30 minutes
**serves:** 4

800 g (1 lb 12 oz) boneless, skinless chicken thighs
1 tablespoon olive oil
1 onion, chopped
1/2 teaspoon ground ginger
2 cinnamon sticks
250 ml (9 fl oz/1 cup) chicken stock
1/4 teaspoon ground saffron threads

4 coriander (cilantro) sprigs, tied in a bunch
zest of 1/2 lemon, removed in wide strips
300 g (101/2 oz/11/3 cups) pitted prunes
2 tablespoons honey
1 tablespoon sesame seeds, toasted

- Trim the chicken of any fat, then cut each thigh into quarters. Heat the oil in a 6 litre (210 fl oz) pressure cooker over medium–high heat and cook the chicken in batches until well browned. Remove from the cooker and set aside. Add the onion to the cooker and cook over medium heat for 5 minutes or until starting to soften. Add the ginger and cinnamon sticks and cook for a further 1 minute or until aromatic.

- Return the chicken to the cooker with the stock, saffron and coriander sprigs. Stir well. Lock the lid in place and bring the cooker to high pressure over high heat. Once high pressure is reached, reduce the heat to stabilise the pressure and cook for 6 minutes or until the chicken is tender. Remove the cooker from the heat and release the pressure using the natural release method. Remove the lid carefully.

- Add the strips of lemon zest, prunes and honey and simmer, uncovered, for 5 minutes or until the sauce has reduced slightly and the prunes have started to collapse. Remove and discard the coriander sprigs. Serve sprinkled with sesame seeds.

# CREAMY CHICKEN CURRY

**preparation time:** 20 minutes (+ 2 hours marinating)
**cooking time:** 15 minutes
**serves:** 4

2 cm (3/4 inch) piece ginger, chopped
3 garlic cloves, roughly chopped
1 kg (2 lb 4 oz) boneless, skinless
   chicken thighs
70 g (2¹/2 oz/¹/2 cup) blanched
   almonds
150 g (5¹/2 oz) Greek-style yoghurt
¹/2 teaspoon chilli powder
¹/4 teaspoon ground cloves
¹/4 teaspoon ground cinnamon

1 teaspoon garam masala
4 cardamom pods, lightly crushed
1 x 400 g (14 oz) tin chopped
   tomatoes
1 large onion, thinly sliced
125 ml (4 fl oz/¹/2 cup) chicken stock
80 ml (2¹/2 fl oz/¹/3 cup) thick
   (double/heavy) cream
1 handful coriander (cilantro) leaves,
   finely chopped

▶

► ● Using a mortar and pestle or a food processor, crush or blend the ginger and garlic together to form a paste. Alternatively, finely grate the ginger and crush the garlic and then mix them together.

● Trim the chicken of excess fat, then cut into large pieces. Set aside while you prepare the marinade.

● Grind the almonds in a food processor or finely chop them with a knife. Put the ginger and garlic paste and almonds in a large bowl with the yoghurt, chilli powder, cloves, cinnamon, garam masala, cardamom pods, tomatoes and 1 teaspoon salt. Blend together with a fork. Add the chicken pieces and stir to coat the chicken thoroughly. Cover and marinate in the refrigerator for 2 hours or overnight.

● Combine the chicken mixture with the onion and stock in a 6 litre (210 fl oz) pressure cooker. Bring to a simmer over high heat, then stir well. Lock the lid in place and bring the cooker to high pressure over high heat. Once high pressure is reached, reduce the heat to stabilise the pressure and cook for 6 minutes or until the chicken is tender.

● Remove the cooker from the heat and release the pressure using the natural release method. Remove the lid carefully.

● Stir in the cream and half the coriander and heat through. Season to taste with salt and freshly ground black pepper. Sprinkle the chicken with the remaining coriander and serve with rice.

# BASQUE CHICKEN

**preparation time:** 15 minutes
**cooking time:** 40 minutes
**serves:** 4

1.8 kg (4 lb) chicken (see Note)
1 tablespoon olive oil
1 onion, cut into 2 cm (3/4 inch) dice
200 g (7 oz) chorizo sausage, sliced
1 red capsicum (pepper), cut into
    2 cm (3/4 inch) dice
1 green capsicum (pepper), cut into
    2 cm (3/4 inch) dice
2 garlic cloves, finely chopped

150 ml (5 fl oz) white wine
250 ml (9 fl oz/1 cup) chicken stock
60 g (2 1/4 oz/1/4 cup) tomato paste
    (concentrated purée)
1/4 preserved lemon
90 g (3 1/4 oz/1/2 cup) black olives
2 tablespoons chopped basil
2 tablespoons chopped flat-leaf
    (Italian) parsley

• Joint the chicken into eight pieces by removing both legs and cutting between the joint of the drumstick and the thigh. Cut down either side of the backbone and lift it out. Turn the chicken over and cut through the cartilage down the centre of the breastbone. Cut each breast in half, leaving the wing attached to the top half.

• Heat the oil in a 6 litre (210 fl oz) pressure cooker over medium–high heat and cook the chicken in batches until well browned. Remove and set aside.

• Add the onion and chorizo to the cooker and cook over medium heat for 10 minutes or until the onion is soft. Remove from the cooker with a slotted spoon and set aside. Drain the excess oil from the cooker.

• Return the chicken pieces to the cooker with the onion mixture, red and green capsicums, garlic, wine, stock and tomato paste. Bring to the boil over high heat, then stir well. Lock the lid in place and bring the cooker to high pressure over high heat. Once high pressure is reached, reduce the heat to stabilise the pressure and cook for 8 minutes or until the chicken is tender.

► ● Remove the cooker from the heat and release the pressure using the natural release method. Remove the lid carefully.

● Rinse the preserved lemon well, remove and discard the pulp and membrane and finely dice the rind. Add to the chicken with the olives and simmer, uncovered, until the sauce has reduced to the desired consistency and flavour.

● Stir through the basil and serve sprinkled with the parsley. Serve with rice if desired.

*Note* *Alternatively, buy 1.8 kg (4 lb) chicken pieces.*

# CHICKEN BRAISED WITH GINGER AND STAR ANISE

**preparation time:** 10 minutes
**cooking time:** 15–20 minutes
**serves:** 4

1 kg (2 lb 4 oz) boneless, skinless chicken thighs
1 teaspoon sichuan peppercorns
3 cm x 2 cm (1$^{1}$/$_4$ inch x $^3$/$_4$ inch) piece ginger, shredded
2 garlic cloves, chopped
250 ml (9 fl oz/1 cup) chicken stock

80 ml (2$^{1}$/$_2$ fl oz/$^1$/$_3$ cup) Chinese rice wine
60 ml (2 fl oz/$^1$/$_4$ cup) light soy sauce
1 tablespoon honey
1 star anise
3 spring onions (scallions), thinly sliced diagonally

- Trim the chicken of excess fat, then cut each thigh in half. Put the chicken pieces, peppercorns, ginger, garlic, stock, rice wine, soy sauce, honey and star anise in a 6 litre (210 fl oz) pressure cooker. Lock the lid in place and bring the cooker to high pressure over high heat. Once high pressure is reached, reduce the heat to stabilise the pressure and cook for 6 minutes or until the chicken is tender.

- Remove the cooker from the heat and release the pressure using the natural release method. Remove the lid carefully.

- Using kitchen tongs, remove the chicken from the cooker and set aside in a warm place. Simmer the sauce, uncovered, for 5–10 minutes or until reduced slightly. Season with salt and freshly ground black pepper. Serve the chicken with the sauce and garnished with the spring onions. Serve with steamed rice.

# GREEN CHICKEN CURRY

**preparation time:** 15 minutes
**cooking time:** 25 minutes
**serves:** 4–6

750 g (1 lb 10 oz) boneless, skinless
  chicken thighs
2–3 tablespoons peanut oil
5 long, thin eggplants (aubergines),
  cut into 1.5 cm (5/8 inch) slices
2 tablespoons green curry paste
250 ml (9 fl oz/1 cup) chicken stock
1 x 185 ml (6 fl oz) tin coconut milk
7 kaffir lime leaves, torn in half

2 teaspoons fish sauce, or to taste
1 tablespoon grated palm sugar
  (jaggery) or soft brown sugar
1 handful Thai sweet basil leaves,
  to garnish
1 long green chilli, seeded and thinly
  sliced, to garnish

*Chicken*

▶

▶ ● Trim the chicken of excess fat, then cut each thigh into 3 cm (1 1/4 inch) pieces.

● Heat 1–2 tablespoons of the oil in a 6 litre (210 fl oz) pressure cooker over medium–high heat and cook the eggplant in batches until browned. Remove from the cooker and set aside.

● Heat another tablespoon of oil in the cooker over medium–high heat and cook the chicken in batches until well browned. Remove from the cooker and set aside.

● Add the curry paste to the cooker and cook over medium heat for 1–2 minutes or until aromatic. Return the chicken to the cooker and stir to coat in the paste. Add the stock, coconut milk, eggplant and four of the lime leaves. Lock the lid in place and bring the cooker to high pressure over high heat. Once high pressure is reached, reduce the heat to stabilise the pressure and cook for 6 minutes or until the chicken is tender.

● Remove the cooker from the heat and release the pressure using the natural release method. Remove the lid carefully.

● Stir through the fish sauce, brown sugar and remaining lime leaves. Garnish with basil and chilli and serve with steamed rice.

# PENANG CHICKEN CURRY

preparation time: 20 minutes
cooking time: 10 minutes
serves: 4

800 g (1 lb 12 oz) boneless, skinless
   chicken breasts
1 tablespoon peanut oil
250 ml (9 fl oz/1 cup) chicken stock
1 x 185 ml (6 fl oz) tin coconut cream
coriander (cilantro) leaves,
   to garnish
sliced red chilli, to garnish

### RED CURRY PASTE

1 red onion, thickly sliced
10 g ($^1$/4 oz) galangal, sliced
2 garlic cloves, chopped
1 teaspoon chilli powder
2 coriander (cilantro) roots,
   washed well
1 teaspoon shrimp paste
40 g (1$^1$/2 oz/$^1$/4 cup) peanuts, toasted

● To make the red curry paste, place all the paste ingredients in a food processor and blend until smooth. Alternatively, pound the ingredients using a mortar and pestle to form a smooth paste.

● Trim the chicken of excess fat, then cut into 2 cm ( $^3$/4 inch) pieces. Cover and set aside.

● Heat the oil in a 6 litre (210 fl oz) pressure cooker over medium heat and cook the curry paste for 3 minutes or until aromatic. Add the chicken and stir to coat in the paste. Stir in the stock and coconut cream. Lock the lid in place and bring the cooker to high pressure over high heat. Once high pressure is reached, reduce the heat to stabilise the pressure and cook for 5 minutes or until the chicken is tender. Remove the cooker from the heat and release the pressure using the quick release method. Remove the lid carefully.

● Ladle the curry into large serving bowls and garnish with the coriander and chilli. Serve with jasmine rice.

# BUTTER CHICKEN

**preparation time:** 15 minutes
**cooking time:** 35 minutes
**serves:** 6

1 kg (2 lb 4 oz) boneless, skinless
   chicken thighs
1 tablespoon peanut oil
2 teaspoons garam masala
2 teaspoons sweet paprika
2 teaspoons ground coriander
1 tablespoon grated fresh ginger
1/4 teaspoon chilli powder
1 cinnamon stick

6 cardamom pods, bruised
375 g (13 oz/1 1/2 cups) tomato
   passata (puréed tomatoes)
125 ml (4 fl oz/1/2 cup) chicken stock
60 g (2 1/4 oz/1/4 cup) plain yoghurt
1 tablespoon cornflour (cornstarch)
1 tablespoon sugar
125 ml (4 fl oz/1/2 cup) pouring cream
1 tablespoon lemon juice

• Trim the chicken of excess fat, then cut each thigh into quarters. Heat the oil in a
6 litre (210 fl oz) pressure cooker over medium–high heat and cook the chicken in
batches until well browned. Remove from the cooker and set aside.

• Add the garam masala, paprika, coriander, ginger, chilli powder, cinnamon stick and
cardamom pods to the cooker and cook over medium heat for 4 minutes or until
aromatic. Return the chicken to the cooker and stir to coat in the spices. Add the
tomato passata and stock and bring to the boil over high heat. Stir well. Lock the lid
in place and bring the cooker to high pressure over high heat. Once high pressure is
reached, reduce the heat to stabilise the pressure and cook for 6 minutes or until the
chicken is tender. Remove the cooker from the heat and release the pressure using
the natural release method. Remove the lid carefully.

• Combine the yoghurt with the cornflour. Add the yoghurt mixture to the cooker
along with the sugar, cream and lemon juice. Stir over low heat, uncovered, for
4–5 minutes or until the sauce thickens slightly. Serve with steamed rice.

# MILD CURRY OF CHICKEN, SWEET POTATOES AND SPLIT PEAS

preparation time: 15 minutes (+ overnight soaking)
cooking time: 35 minutes
serves: 4-6

220 g (7³/4 oz/1 cup) dried yellow split peas
6 boneless, skinless chicken thighs
2 tablespoons vegetable oil
1 red onion, chopped
2 garlic cloves, crushed
1 tablespoon grated fresh ginger
3 teaspoons curry powder
500 ml (17 fl oz/2 cups) chicken stock

1 x 400 g (14 oz) tin chopped tomatoes
500 g (1 lb 2 oz) orange sweet potato, cut into 2 cm (³/4 inch) cubes
125 ml (4 fl oz/¹/2 cup) pouring cream
1 small handful coriander (cilantro) leaves, chopped

● Put the split peas in a bowl, cover with plenty of water and soak for several hours or overnight. Drain.

● Trim the chicken of excess fat. Heat half the oil in a 6 litre (210 fl oz) pressure cooker over medium–high heat and cook the chicken in batches until well browned. Remove from the cooker and set aside. Heat the remaining oil in the cooker and cook the onion for 8 minutes or until softened. Add the garlic, ginger and curry powder and cook for 2–3 minutes or until aromatic.

● Add the drained split peas, stock and tomatoes to the cooker and stir well. Lock the lid in place and bring the cooker to high pressure over high heat. Once high pressure is reached, reduce the heat to stabilise the pressure and cook for 5 minutes. Remove the cooker from the heat and release the pressure using the quick release method. Remove the lid carefully.

▶

*Chicken*

▶ ● Add the chicken and sweet potato to the cooker, replace the lid immediately and lock in place. Bring the cooker back to high pressure over high heat. Once high pressure is reached, reduce the heat to stabilise the pressure and cook for a further 5 minutes or until the split peas, chicken and sweet potato are cooked and tender.

● Remove the cooker from the heat again and release the pressure using the natural release method. Remove the lid carefully.

● Stir the cream and coriander through the curry and heat gently, uncovered, until warmed through. Serve with steamed beans and basmati rice or Indian flat bread.

## CHICKEN GOULASH

**preparation time:** 20 minutes
**cooking time:** 30 minutes
**serves:** 4

700 g (1 lb 9 oz) boneless, skinless
   chicken thighs
1 tablespoon olive oil
1 onion, sliced
2 garlic cloves, sliced
1 tablespoon sweet paprika
125 ml (4 fl oz/$^1$/$_2$ cup) dry white wine
250 ml (9 fl oz/1 cup) chicken stock
125 g (4$^1$/$_2$ oz/$^1$/$_2$ cup) tomato passata
   (puréed tomatoes)

2 green capsicums (peppers), seeded
   and sliced
1 marjoram sprig
125 g (4$^1$/$_2$ oz/$^1$/$_2$ cup) sour cream
   or crème fraîche
1 small handful flat-leaf (Italian)
   parsley

● Trim the chicken of excess fat, then cut each thigh into quarters. Heat the oil in a 6 litre (210 fl oz) pressure cooker over medium–high heat and cook the chicken in batches until well browned. Remove from the cooker and set aside.

- Add the onion to the cooker and cook over medium heat for 10 minutes or until softened. Add the garlic and paprika and cook for 1 minute or until aromatic. Add the wine and simmer for 2 minutes, scraping the base of the pot.

- Return the chicken to the cooker with the stock, tomato passata, capsicum and marjoram. Bring to the boil over high heat. Lock the lid in place and bring the cooker to high pressure over high heat. Once high pressure is reached, reduce the heat to stabilise the pressure and cook for 5 minutes or until the chicken is tender. Remove the cooker from the heat and release the pressure using the natural release method. Remove the lid carefully.

- Stir the sour cream into the chicken mixture. Cook, uncovered, over low heat until heated through (do not boil). Season to taste with salt and freshly ground black pepper and stir through the parsley. Serve with rice.

# ARROZ CON POLLO

preparation time: 15 minutes
cooking time: 35 minutes
serves: 6–8

4 very ripe tomatoes
1 tablespoon olive oil
2 kg (4 lb 8 oz) chicken pieces,
  skin removed
1 large onion, finely chopped
200 g (7 oz) chorizo sausage, sliced
2 green or red capsicums (peppers),
  seeded and diced
1 tablespoon sweet paprika
1 tablespoon smoked paprika
1 long red chilli, seeded and chopped

2 garlic cloves, crushed
80 ml (2$^1$/2 fl oz/$^1$/3 cup) sherry
1.5 litres (52 fl oz/6 cups) chicken
  stock
440 g (15$^1$/2 oz/2 cups) arborio rice
$^1$/2 teaspoon saffron threads
100 g (3$^1$/2 oz/$^2$/3 cup) frozen peas
2$^1$/2 tablespoons tomato paste
  (concentrated purée)
1 small handful flat-leaf (Italian)
  parsley, finely chopped

● Score a cross in the base of each tomato. Put the tomatoes in a heatproof bowl and cover with boiling water. Leave for 30 seconds, then transfer to cold water, drain and peel the skin away from the cross. Cut the tomatoes in half, scoop out the seeds with a teaspoon and discard them, and roughly chop the flesh.

● Heat the oil in an 8 litre (280 fl oz) pressure cooker over medium–high heat and cook the chicken in batches until well browned. Remove and set aside.

● Add the onion and chorizo to the cooker and cook over medium heat for 5 minutes or until the onion starts to soften. Add the capsicum, sweet and smoked paprika, chilli and garlic and cook for a further 2 minutes or until aromatic.

● Add the sherry to the cooker and simmer for 2 minutes, scraping the base of the pot. Add the chicken, chopped tomato, stock, rice and saffron to the cooker and stir well. Lock the lid in place and bring the cooker to high pressure over high heat. Once high pressure is reached, reduce the heat to stabilise the pressure and cook for 6 minutes or until the chicken is cooked and the rice is tender but firm to the bite.

● Remove the cooker from the heat and release the pressure using the natural release method. Remove the lid carefully.

● Stir in the peas and tomato paste and cook, uncovered, over medium heat for 2 minutes or until the peas are tender. Stir in the parsley and season to taste with salt and freshly ground black pepper. Serve immediately.

# CHICKEN COOKED IN WHITE WINE

preparation time: 20 minutes
cooking time: 30 minutes
serves: 4

40 g (1¹/2 oz/¹/2 cup) fresh
   breadcrumbs
4 garlic cloves, crushed
2 teaspoons finely chopped rosemary
1 teaspoon finely grated lemon zest

1.5 kg (3 lb 5 oz) chicken
1 bay leaf
3 thyme sprigs
400 ml (14 fl oz) chicken stock
200 ml (7 fl oz) dry white wine

- In a small bowl, combine the breadcrumbs, garlic, rosemary and lemon zest to make the stuffing.

- Rinse the chicken inside and out and pat dry with paper towel. Loosely stuff the body cavity of the chicken with the stuffing, then tie or skewer the legs together to secure the stuffing inside the chicken.

- Put the chicken, breast side down, in an 8 litre (280 fl oz) pressure cooker with the bay leaf and thyme. Pour over the stock, wine and 125 ml (4 fl oz/¹/2 cup) water. Bring to the boil over high heat. Lock the lid in place and bring the cooker to high pressure over high heat. Once high pressure is reached, reduce the heat to stabilise the pressure and cook for 25 minutes or until the chicken is tender.

- Remove the cooker from the heat and release the pressure using the natural release method. Remove the lid carefully.

- Carve the chicken into pieces and serve with the pan juices. Serve with steamed buttered potatoes and green vegetables if desired.

# HOWTOWDIE

**preparation time:** 25 minutes
**cooking time:** 55 minutes
**serves:** 4–6

1.8 kg (4 lb) chicken
1 leek, white part only, sliced
1 bay leaf
very small pinch ground cloves
pinch freshly grated nutmeg
500 ml (17 fl oz/2 cups) chicken stock
2 chicken livers, chopped
60 ml (2 fl oz/¼ cup) thick
    (double/heavy) cream

**STUFFING**
85 g (3 oz/⅔ cup) oatmeal
2 tablespoons shredded suet or
    dripping (see Note)
1 small onion, finely chopped
2 tablespoons chopped flat-leaf
    (Italian) parsley
1 teaspoon finely grated lemon zest
2 tablespoons whisky

- To make the stuffing, toast the oatmeal in a frying pan over medium heat until golden and aromatic. Transfer to a bowl. Increase the heat to medium–high, add the suet to the pan and, when it is bubbling, add the onion and cook for 10 minutes, or until soft and lightly golden. Add the onion to the bowl with the oatmeal along with the parsley, lemon zest and whisky. Stir to combine so that the mixture is loosely bound. If it is too dry, add 1 tablespoon water or chicken stock. Season well with salt and freshly ground black pepper and allow to cool completely before stuffing the chicken.

- Rinse the chicken inside and out and pat dry with paper towel. Loosely fill the cavity with the stuffing, then tie or skewer the legs together to secure the stuffing inside.

- Put the chicken in an 8 litre (280 fl oz) pressure cooker along with the leek, bay leaf, cloves, nutmeg and stock. Season with salt and freshly ground black pepper. Bring to the boil over high heat. Lock the lid in place and bring the cooker to high pressure over high heat. Once high pressure is reached, reduce the heat to stabilise the pressure and cook for 30 minutes or until the chicken is tender.

*Chicken*

- Remove the cooker from the heat and release the pressure using the natural release method. Remove the lid carefully. Lift the chicken out of the cooker, transfer it to a plate and cover to keep warm while you finish the sauce.

- Purée the chicken livers in the small bowl of a food processor. Remove all but 250 ml (9 fl oz/1 cup) of liquid from the pressure cooker. Add the puréed chicken livers to the liquid left in the cooker and stir until they melt into the sauce. Add the cream and cook, uncovered, over low heat for 2 minutes, or until the sauce is heated through, but don't allow it to boil. (For a smoother sauce, strain the cooking liquid before adding the livers and cream.)

- Serve the chicken whole or carved with the sauce poured over it and a little of the stuffing on the side. Serve with green vegetables such as blanched green beans and wilted spinach.

*note Howtowdie is a traditional Scottish recipe of roast chicken with oat stuffing. Suet is a firm, white fat available from most butchers.*

# CHICKEN WITH TARRAGON AND FENNEL

**preparation time:** 20 minutes
**cooking time:** 50 minutes
**serves:** 4

| | |
|---|---|
| 1 large fennel bulb | 300 ml (10½ fl oz) chicken stock |
| 1 red onion | 60 ml (2 fl oz/¼ cup) verjuice |
| 1.8 kg (4 lb) chicken | 600 g (1 lb 5 oz) kipfler potatoes |
| 1 lemon | 250 g (9 oz) cherry tomatoes |
| 2 tablespoons extra virgin olive oil | 2 tablespoons chopped flat-leaf |
| 4 garlic cloves, peeled | (Italian) parsley |
| 3 tarragon sprigs | |

▶

▶ ● Remove the tough outer layer of the fennel. Slice into 8–10 wedges, leaving the root section attached so each fennel wedge doesn't fall apart. Peel the onion and cut it into 8–10 wedges, again using the root section to hold the wedges together.

● Rinse the chicken inside and out and pat dry with paper towel. Cut the lemon in half and place in the chicken cavity. Season the chicken with salt and freshly ground black pepper and set aside.

● Heat half the oil in an 8 litre (280 fl oz) pressure cooker over medium heat and cook the fennel and onion wedges, in batches if necessary, for 5 minutes or until lightly golden brown. Remove from the cooker and set aside.

● Heat the remaining oil in the cooker over medium–high heat. Add the whole chicken and cook, turning until browned all over.

● Turn the chicken, breast side up, and add the garlic cloves and tarragon to the cooker. Pour over the stock and verjuice and season with salt and pepper. Lock the lid in place and bring the cooker to high pressure over high heat. Once high pressure is reached, reduce the heat to stabilise the pressure and cook for 20 minutes.

● Meanwhile, peel the potatoes and cut into 2 cm (3/4 inch) pieces. Cover with water and set aside.

● Remove the cooker from the heat and release the pressure using the quick release method. Remove the lid carefully.

● Add the onion and fennel, drained potatoes and the tomatoes, placing them around and on top of the chicken, then replace the lid immediately and lock in place. Bring the cooker back to high pressure over high heat. Once high pressure is reached, reduce the heat to stabilise the pressure and cook for a further 10 minutes.

● Remove the cooker from the heat and release the pressure using the natural release method. Remove the lid carefully. Carve the chicken and serve with the vegetables and pan juices, and sprinkle with chopped parsley.

*Chicken*

# DRUNKEN CHICKEN WITH RICE

preparation time: 15 minutes
cooking time: 25 minutes
serves: 4

1.5 kg (3 lb 5 oz) chicken thigh
    pieces
2 tablespoons olive oil
2 slices fresh ginger
2 garlic cloves, squashed
1 star anise
200 g (7 oz/1 cup) jasmine rice

2 spring onions (scallions), trimmed
250 ml (9 fl oz/1 cup) hot chicken
    stock
185 ml (6 fl oz/3/4 cup) Chinese rice
    wine
light soy sauce, to serve

• Trim the chicken pieces of excess fat, then season with salt and freshly ground black pepper. Heat the oil in a 6 litre (210 fl oz) pressure cooker over medium–high heat and cook the chicken in batches until well browned. Remove from the cooker and set aside.

• Reduce the heat to medium, add the ginger, garlic and star anise to the cooker and cook for 2 minutes or until aromatic. Add the rice and spring onions and stir until the rice is coated with the oil.

• Return the chicken pieces to the cooker, pushing them about halfway into the rice. Pour over the hot stock and rice wine. Lock the lid in place and bring the cooker to high pressure over high heat. Once high pressure is reached, reduce the heat to stabilise the pressure and cook for 6 minutes or until the chicken and rice are cooked.

• Remove the cooker from the heat and release the pressure using the natural release method. Remove the lid carefully. Serve the chicken drizzled with the light soy sauce.

*Chicken*

# Beef & Veal

Beef curries, casseroles and braises
can be on the table in no time at all
when prepared in a pressure cooker.

# BEEF PHO

**preparation time:** 25 minutes
**cooking time:** 1 hour 5 minutes
**serves:** 6

750 g (1 lb 10 oz) beef shin bones
750 ml (26 fl oz/3 cups) beef stock
10 cm (4 inch) piece ginger, thinly
    sliced
8 French shallots, peeled and halved
6 black peppercorns
2 star anise
1 cinnamon stick
4 cloves
6 coriander seeds
2 teaspoons sugar
500 g (1 lb 2 oz) piece skirt steak
2 tablespoons fish sauce
500 g (1 lb 2 oz) fresh thin rice
    noodles

150 g (5$^1$/$_2$ oz) rump steak, very
    thinly sliced
3 spring onions (scallions), finely
    chopped
$^1$/$_4$ cup coriander (cilantro) leaves
chilli sauce or hoisin sauce, to serve

**GARNISHES**
red chillies, sliced
bean sprouts
basil leaves
spring onions (scallions), sliced
    diagonally
lime wedges

*Beef & veal*

● Put the shin bones in a 6 litre (210 fl oz) pressure cooker and cover with cold water. Bring to the boil over high heat. Drain, discarding the water. Rinse the bones under cold running water and wash out the pressure cooker pot.

● Return the shin bones to the cooker with the stock, 1.5 litres (52 fl oz/6 cups) water, ginger, French shallots, peppercorns, star anise, cinnamon stick, cloves, coriander seeds, sugar and 1 teaspoon salt. Lock the lid in place and bring the cooker to high pressure over high heat. Once high pressure is reached, reduce the heat to stabilise the pressure and cook for 20 minutes.

▶

► ● Remove the cooker from the heat and release the pressure using the quick release method. Remove the lid carefully. Add the skirt steak, replace the lid immediately and lock in place. Bring the cooker back to high pressure over high heat. Once high pressure is reached, reduce the heat to stabilise the pressure and cook for 35 minutes or until the steak is very tender.

● Remove the cooker from the heat and release the pressure using the natural release method. Remove the lid carefully. Using kitchen tongs, remove the beef to a board and allow to cool slightly. When the beef is cool enough to touch, cut it across the grain into very thin slices. Set aside.

● Strain the stock, then return the stock to the cooker, discarding the bones and spices. Stir the fish sauce into the stock.

● Place the noodles in a heatproof bowl, cover with boiling water and soak for 3 minutes or until tender, then drain. Bring the stock in the pressure cooker back to the boil.

● Divide the noodles among the serving bowls. Place some slices of the cooked beef and a few slices of the raw steak on top of the noodles in each bowl. Ladle the hot stock over the top and sprinkle with the spring onion and coriander.

● Arrange the garnishes on a platter in the centre of the table for each person to choose from. Serve with chilli sauce or hoisin sauce to add to the soup if desired.

*Beef & veal*

# BORSCHT BEEF

**preparation time:** 20 minutes
**cooking time:** 55 minutes
**serves:** 4–6

1.2 kg (2 lb 10 oz) chuck steak
1 tablespoon olive oil
1 onion, cut into 2 cm (3/4 inch) dice
2 celery stalks, cut into 2 cm
   (3/4 inch) dice
2 beetroot (beets), peeled and cut
   into 3 cm (1¼ inch) dice
375 ml (13 fl oz/1½ cups) beef stock
1 x 400 g (14 oz) tin chopped
   tomatoes

60 g (2¼ oz/¼ cup) tomato paste
   (concentrated purée)
2 tablespoons vinegar
½ small cabbage, cut into 2 cm
   (3/4 inch) dice
125 g (4½ oz/½ cup) sour cream
2 tablespoons prepared horseradish
squeeze of lemon juice
2 tablespoons chopped flat-leaf
   (Italian) parsley, to garnish

● Trim the beef of fat and cut it into 2 cm (3/4 inch) cubes. Heat the oil in a 6 litre (210 fl oz) pressure cooker over medium–high heat and cook the beef in batches until well browned. Remove from the cooker and set aside. Add the onion and celery to the cooker and cook over medium heat for 10 minutes or until the onion softens.

● Return the beef to the cooker with the beetroot, stock, tomatoes, tomato paste and vinegar and bring to a simmer over high heat. Lock the lid in place and bring to high pressure over high heat. Once high pressure is reached, reduce the heat to stabilise the pressure and cook for 25 minutes.

● Remove the cooker from the heat and release the pressure using the natural release method. Remove the lid carefully. Stir in the cabbage and simmer, uncovered, for 5 minutes or until the cabbage is tender.

● Combine the sour cream, horseradish and lemon juice in a bowl and season with salt. Serve the soup garnished with the horseradish cream and parsley.

*Beef & veal*

# SUKIYAKI SOUP

**preparation time:** 20 minutes
**cooking time:** 15 minutes
**serves:** 4–6

1 teaspoon dashi granules
1 leek, white part only
20 g (3/4 oz) dried shiitake
    mushrooms, sliced
1.5 litres (52 fl oz/6 cups) chicken
    stock
125 ml (4 fl oz/1/2 cup) soy sauce
2 tablespoons mirin
1 1/2 tablespoons sugar

100 g (3 1/2 oz) dried rice vermicelli
    noodles
100 g (3 1/2 oz) Chinese cabbage,
    shredded
400 g (14 oz) rump steak, thinly
    sliced
300 g (10 1/2 oz) silken firm tofu, cut
    into 2 cm (3/4 inch) cubes
6 spring onions (scallions), sliced
    diagonally

● Put the dashi in a heatproof bowl with 500 ml (17 fl oz/2 cups) boiling water and stir until the granules have dissolved.

● Leave the root attached to the leek and slice in half lengthways. Wash thoroughly under cold water to remove any grit, then drain. Thinly slice the leek, discarding the root.

● Put the dashi, leek, shiitake mushrooms, stock, soy sauce, mirin and sugar in a 6 litre (210 fl oz) pressure cooker. Lock the lid in place and bring the cooker to high pressure over high heat. Once high pressure is reached, reduce the heat to stabilise the pressure and cook for 10 minutes.

● Meanwhile, place the vermicelli in a heatproof bowl, cover with boiling water and soak for 10 minutes or until softened, then drain.

● Remove the cooker from the heat and release the pressure using the natural release method. Remove the lid carefully.

*Beef & veal*

- Add the cabbage to the cooker and simmer gently, uncovered, for 2 minutes. Remove the cooker from the heat, add the beef and tofu and stand for 2 minutes. Divide the noodles among the serving bowls and ladle over the soup. Serve garnished with the spring onion.

# GREEK-STYLE STUFFED EGGPLANT

**preparation time:** 25 minutes
**cooking time:** 15 minutes
**serves:** 4

2 large eggplants (aubergines)
1 onion, finely chopped
2 garlic cloves, chopped
350 g (12 oz) minced (ground) beef
   or lamb
60 g (2¹/₄ oz/¹/₄ cup) tomato paste
   (concentrated purée)
2 tablespoons chopped flat-leaf
   (Italian) parsley

100 ml (3¹/₂ fl oz) red wine
1 x 400 g (14 oz) tin chopped
   tomatoes
100 ml (3¹/₂ fl oz) chicken stock
2 bay leaves
1 cinnamon stick
1 tablespoon dried oregano
Greek-style yoghurt, to serve

- Halve the eggplants lengthways. Use a sharp knife to cut into the flesh, about 1 cm (¹/₂ inch) in from the edge. Use a large spoon to scoop out the eggplant flesh leaving the 1 cm boarder, then roughly chop the flesh.

- Place the eggplant flesh in a bowl along with the onion, garlic, beef, tomato paste and parsley. Season with salt and freshly ground black pepper and mix well to combine.

- Stuff the beef mixture into the hole in the eggplants, reserving any leftover stuffing. Put the wine, tomatoes, stock, bay leaves, cinnamon stick, oregano and any remaining eggplant stuffing in a 6 litre (210 fl oz) pressure cooker. Stir well. Place the stuffed ▶

*Beef & veal*

▶ eggplants into a steamer basket or onto a trivet and place into the cooker over the tomato mixture. Bring to the boil over high heat. Lock the lid in place and bring the cooker to low pressure over high heat. Once low pressure is reached, reduce the heat to stabilise the pressure and cook for 8 minutes. Remove the cooker from the heat and release the pressure using the natural release method. Remove the lid carefully.

● Remove the eggplants to a serving platter. Season the sauce with salt and freshly ground black pepper. Serve the eggplants with the sauce, topped with a dollop of yoghurt and a Greek salad on the side.

# ITALIAN MEATBALLS WITH TOMATO SAUCE

**preparation time:** 20 minutes (+ 20 minutes refrigeration)
**cooking time:** 10 minutes
**serves:** 4–6

700 g (1 lb 9 oz) tomato passata
   (puréed tomatoes)
125 ml (4 fl oz/$^1$/$_2$ cup) red wine
chopped flat-leaf (Italian) parsley,
   to serve

## MEATBALLS
1 onion, finely chopped
80 g (2$^3$/$_4$ oz/$^1$/$_2$ cup) pine nuts,
   roughly chopped
2 garlic cloves, crushed

1 small handful flat-leaf (Italian)
   parsley, roughly chopped
1 teaspoon chopped rosemary
2 teaspoons fennel seeds, ground
55 g (2 oz/$^2$/$_3$ cup) fresh breadcrumbs
25 g (1 oz/$^1$/$_4$ cup) freshly grated
   parmesan cheese
finely grated zest of 1 large lemon
500 g (1 lb 2 oz) minced (ground)
   beef or pork

● To make the meatballs, combine all the ingredients in a bowl. Use your hands to mix well. Roll the mixture into walnut-sized balls and place on a tray. Refrigerate the meatballs for 20 minutes.

*Beef & veal*

- Put the tomato passata, wine and 125 ml (4 fl oz/$^1$/$_2$ cup) water in a 6 litre (210 fl oz) pressure cooker. Season with salt and freshly ground black pepper. Bring to a simmer over high heat and then add the meatballs. Lock the lid in place and bring the cooker to low pressure over high heat. Once low pressure is reached, reduce the heat to stabilise the pressure and cook for 5 minutes or until the meatballs are cooked through.

- Remove the cooker from the heat and release the pressure using the natural release method. Remove the lid carefully.

- Serve the meatballs and tomato sauce sprinkled with the parsley. Serve with spaghetti, rice or mashed potatoes, and a side salad.

# VEAL OLIVES WITH PROSCIUTTO, CHEESE AND SAGE

preparation time: 20 minutes
cooking time: 15 minutes
serves: 4

6 x 150 g (5$^1$/$_2$ oz) veal leg steaks
   (schnitzels)
6 prosciutto slices, trimmed of fat
50 g (1$^3$/$_4$ oz/$^1$/$_2$ cup) freshly grated
   parmesan cheese
finely grated zest of 1 lemon
12 sage leaves, plus extra, to garnish
1 tablespoon olive oil
20 g ($^3$/$_4$ oz) butter

**TOMATO AND OLIVE SAUCE**
1 x 400 g (14 oz) tin chopped
   tomatoes
125 ml (4 fl oz/$^1$/$_2$ cup) chicken stock
30 g (1 oz) semi-dried (sun-blushed)
   tomatoes, chopped
2 spring onions (scallions), chopped
2 garlic cloves, crushed
10 black olives, pitted and chopped
1 teaspoon caster (superfine) sugar

*Beef & veal*

▶

▶ • To make the tomato and olive sauce, combine the tomatoes, stock, semi-dried tomatoes, spring onion, garlic, olives and sugar in a bowl. Season with salt and freshly ground black pepper. Set the sauce aside.

• Put each veal steak between two sheets of plastic wrap and use the flat side of a meat mallet to pound them to about 5 mm (1/4 inch) thick and roughly 25 cm x 10 cm (10 inches x 4 inches) in size.

• Lay the prosciutto slices over the top of each veal steak. Evenly divide the parmesan, lemon zest and sage leaves over each piece of veal. Season with freshly ground black pepper. Roll up the veal to enclose the prosciutto, parmesan, lemon zest and sage and secure with a toothpick to form veal olives.

• Heat the oil and butter in a 6 litre (210 fl oz) pressure cooker over high heat. When the oil is hot, add the veal olives and cook for 2 minutes, turning frequently, or until well browned on all sides. Remove from the cooker.

• Pour the tomato and olive sauce over the base of the cooker. Arrange the veal olives on the tomato sauce. Bring the sauce to the boil over high heat. Lock the lid in place and bring the cooker to high pressure over high heat. Once high pressure is reached, reduce the heat to stabilise the pressure and cook for 4 minutes. Remove the cooker from the heat and release the pressure using the natural release method. Remove the lid carefully.

• To serve, remove the toothpicks from the veal olives and cut each into three or four thick slices diagonally, then arrange onto serving plates. Pour over the tomato and olive sauce and garnish with an extra sage leaf or two. Serve with mashed potato or polenta and a green vegetable or salad.

Beef & veal

# CHILLI BEEF WITH CAPSICUM, CORIANDER AND AVOCADO

**preparation time:** 20 minutes
**cooking time:** 50 minutes
**serves:** 6

800 g (1 lb 12 oz) chuck steak
2 tablespoons olive oil
2 onions, chopped
1 red capsicum (pepper), seeded and diced
110 g (3³/4 oz) mushroom flats, finely chopped
2 garlic cloves, crushed
4 long green chillies, seeded and finely chopped
2 teaspoons ground cumin
¹/2 teaspoon ground cinnamon
2 bay leaves

2 x 400 g (14 oz) tins chopped tomatoes
300 ml (10¹/2 fl oz) beef stock
1 teaspoon caster (superfine) sugar
1 large handful coriander (cilantro) leaves
1 x 400 g (14 oz) tin red kidney beans, drained, and rinsed (see Note)
25 g (1 oz) dark, bitter chocolate (Mexican if possible), grated
1 firm, ripe avocado
¹/2 red onion, chopped
250 g (9 oz/1 cup) sour cream

*Beef & veal*

• Trim the beef of excess fat, cut into 3 cm (1¹/4 inch) cubes and season with salt and freshly ground black pepper. Heat half the oil in a 6 litre (210 fl oz) pressure cooker over high heat and cook the beef in batches until well browned. Remove from the cooker.

• Add the remaining oil and the onion to the pressure cooker and cook over medium heat for 5 minutes. Add the capsicum and mushrooms and cook for 5 minutes or until the onion is softened. Add the garlic, chillies, cumin, cinnamon and bay leaves and cook for a further 2 minutes or until aromatic.

▶

▶ • Return the beef to the cooker with the tomatoes, stock and sugar and stir well. Lock the lid in place and bring the cooker to high pressure over high heat. Once high pressure is reached, reduce the heat to stabilise the pressure and cook for 25 minutes or until the beef is tender. Remove the cooker from the heat and release the pressure using the natural release method. Remove the lid carefully.

• Add half the coriander, the kidney beans and chocolate to the chilli beef and stir to combine. Season with salt and extra chopped chilli if desired. Cook, uncovered, over medium heat for a further 3 minutes or until the beans are warmed through.

• Meanwhile, chop the avocado and mix with the red onion and remaining coriander. Top the chilli beef with the sour cream and the avocado mixture.

*note* *You can replace the tinned red kidney beans with 250 g (9¹/4 oz/1¹/3 cups) cooked dried red kidney beans (see page 15 for pressure cooking instructions).*

# VEAL WITH PEPERONATA

**preparation time:** 20 minutes
**cooking time:** 35–40 minutes
**serves:** 4

1 x 400 g (14 oz) tin chopped
   tomatoes
1 red onion, cut into thin wedges
2 garlic cloves, chopped
1 red or green chilli, seeded and finely
   chopped (optional)
1 red capsicum (pepper), seeded and
   thinly sliced
1 yellow capsicum (pepper), seeded
   and thinly sliced

1 tablespoon red wine vinegar
1 teaspoon caster (superfine) sugar
125 ml (4 fl oz/¹/2 cup) chicken stock
4 even-sized pieces (about 750 g/
   1 lb 10 oz) veal osso bucco
20 g (³/4 oz) butter
1 tablespoon olive oil
125 ml (4 fl oz/¹/2 cup) dry white wine

**GREMOLATA**
finely grated zest of 1 lemon
1 garlic clove, finely chopped

1 large handful flat-leaf (Italian)
parsley, finely chopped

- To make the peperonata, combine the tomatoes, onion, garlic, chilli, red and yellow capsicum, vinegar, sugar and stock in a bowl. Stir well and season with salt and freshly ground black pepper.

- Trim the osso bucco pieces of excess fat, then season with salt and freshly ground black pepper.

- Heat the butter and oil in an 8 litre (280 fl oz) pressure cooker over medium heat. When hot, add the osso bucco and cook for 2–3 minutes or until well browned on each side. Remove the veal from the cooker and set aside. Add the wine and simmer for 2 minutes, scraping the base of the pot.

- Add half the peperonata to the cooker, arrange the osso bucco on top and then pour the remaining peperonata over. Bring to the boil over high heat. Lock the lid in place and bring the cooker to high pressure over high heat. Once high pressure is reached, reduce the heat to stabilise the pressure and cook for 20–25 minutes or until the osso bucco is very tender.

- Remove the cooker from the heat and release the pressure using the natural release method. Remove the lid carefully.

- Remove the osso bucco from the peperonata, place on a plate and set aside to keep warm. Simmer the peperonata, uncovered, for 5 minutes or until the desired flavour and consistency is reached.

- Meanwhile, to make the gremolata, combine the lemon zest, garlic and parsley in a small bowl.

- Return the osso bucco to the peperonata and heat through. Spoon onto serving plates and sprinkle over the gremolata. Serve with mashed potato or ready-made gnocchi if desired.

*Beef & veal*

# SICHUAN AND ANISE BEEF STEW

**preparation time:** 15 minutes
**cooking time:** 45 minutes
**serves:** 4

1 kg (2 lb 4 oz) chuck steak
2 tablespoons peanut oil
1 large red onion, thickly sliced
2 garlic cloves, crushed
250 ml (9 fl oz/1 cup) red wine
250 ml (9 fl oz/1 cup) beef stock
3 tablespoons tomato paste
   (concentrated purée)
2 bay leaves, crushed

3 long strips orange zest, about
   1.5 cm (5/8 inch) wide
2 star anise
1 teaspoon Sichuan peppercorns
1 tablespoon chopped rosemary
1 teaspoon chopped thyme
1/4 cup chopped coriander
   (cilantro) leaves

● Trim the beef, cut into 3 cm (1 1/4 inch) cubes and season with salt and freshly ground black pepper. Heat 1 tablespoon of the oil in a 6 litre (210 fl oz) pressure cooker over high heat and cook the beef in batches until well browned. Remove from the cooker. Add the remaining oil to the cooker with the onion and cook over medium heat for 5 minutes or until starting to soften. Add the garlic and cook for 1 minute or until aromatic. Add the wine and simmer for 2 minutes, scraping the base of the pot.

● Add the beef, stock, tomato paste, bay leaves, orange zest, star anise, peppercorns, rosemary and thyme to the cooker and stir well. Lock the lid in place and bring the cooker to high pressure over high heat. Once high pressure is reached, reduce the heat to stabilise the pressure and cook for 25 minutes or until the beef is tender.

● Remove the cooker from the heat and release the pressure using the natural release method. Remove the lid carefully.

● Season to taste with salt and freshly ground black pepper. Stir in most of the coriander leaves and garnish with the remainder. Serve with steamed rice.

# VEAL WITH SWEET POTATO, TOMATO AND OLIVES

**preparation time:** 20 minutes
**cooking time:** 55–60 mintues
**serves:** 4

1 kg (2 lb 4 oz) piece veal shoulder
350 g (12 oz) orange sweet potato
2 tablespoons olive oil
1 large red onion, chopped
1 celery stalk, chopped
2 garlic cloves, chopped
60 ml (2 fl oz/¼ cup) white wine
200 ml (7 fl oz) chicken stock

1 x 400 g (14 oz) tin chopped
  tomatoes
2 tablespoons tomato paste
  (concentrated purée)
1 rosemary sprig
12 pitted or stuffed green olives
2 tablespoons chopped parsley
finely grated zest of 1 small lemon

• Cut the veal into 4 cm (1½ inch) cubes. Peel the sweet potato and cut into 4 cm (1½ inch) cubes. Season with salt and freshly ground black pepper.

• Heat half the oil in a 6 litre (210 fl oz) pressure cooker over medium heat and cook the onion, celery and garlic for 5 minutes or until starting to soften. Remove from the cooker and set aside.

• Heat the remaining oil in the cooker over high heat and cook the veal in batches until browned. Remove from the cooker and set aside.

• Add the wine to the cooker and simmer for 2 minutes, scraping the base of the pot. Return the veal and onion mixture to the cooker with 250 ml (9 fl oz/1 cup) water, the stock, sweet potato, tomatoes, tomato paste and rosemary. Bring to the boil over high heat. Lock the lid in place and bring the cooker to low pressure over high heat. Once low pressure is reached, reduce the heat to stabilise the pressure and cook for 25 minutes or until the veal is tender. Remove the rosemary sprig.

▶

*Beef & veal*

77

► ● Remove the cooker from the heat and release the pressure using the natural release method. Remove the lid carefully.

● Return the cooker to the heat and simmer, uncovered, for a further 5–10 minutes or until the sauce has thickened slightly. Stir through the olives and sprinkle with the parsley and lemon zest to serve.

# BRAISED BEEF SHORT RIBS

**preparation time:** 15 minutes
**cooking time:** 50 minutes
**serves:** 6

Beef & veal

2 kg (4 lb 8 oz) beef short ribs
180 g (6$^1$/$_2$ oz) bacon slices
2 tablespoons olive oil
2 onions, chopped
2 garlic cloves, crushed
1 small red chilli, seeded and thinly
   sliced
500 ml (17 fl oz/2 cups) beef stock
1 x 400 g (14 oz) tin chopped
   tomatoes
2 tablespoons tomato paste
   (concentrated purée)

8 bulb spring onions (scallions),
   trimmed
2 strips lemon zest, white pith
   removed
1 teaspoon mild paprika
1 teaspoon chopped rosemary
2 thyme sprigs
1 bay leaf
1 tablespoon soft brown sugar
2 teaspoons Worcestershire sauce
2 tablespoons chopped basil
2 tablespoons chopped flat-leaf
   (Italian) parsley

● Chop the ribs into 4 cm (1$^1$/$_2$ inch) lengths and season well with salt and freshly ground black pepper. Remove the rind and fat from the bacon and cut into small dice.

● Heat half the oil in an 8 litre (280 fl oz) pressure cooker over medium–high heat and cook the bacon for 5 minutes or until crisp. Remove from the cooker and set aside. Add the onion, garlic and chilli and cook over medium heat for 2–3 minutes or until aromatic and the onion is starting to soften. Remove from the cooker and set aside.

● Heat the remaining oil in the cooker over high heat and cook the ribs in batches until well browned. Return all the ribs to the cooker with the bacon, onion mixture, stock, tomatoes, tomato paste, spring onions, strips of lemon zest, paprika, rosemary, thyme, bay leaf, brown sugar and Worcestershire sauce. Stir well.

● Lock the lid in place and bring the cooker to high pressure over high heat. Once high pressure is reached, reduce the heat to stabilise the pressure and cook for 25 minutes or until the ribs are very tender.

● Remove the cooker from the heat and release the pressure using the natural release method. Remove the lid carefully.

● Skim off as much fat as you can from the surface. Stir through the basil and parsley. Serve the ribs with mashed potatoes or soft polenta if desired.

# MEATLOAF WITH TOMATO CHUTNEY SAUCE

preparation time: 25 minutes
cooking time: 15 minutes
serves: 4–6

cooking oil spray, to grease

## TOMATO CHUTNEY SAUCE
1 x 400 g (14 oz) tin chopped tomatoes
250 g (9 oz/1 cup) tomato sauce
   (ketchup)

2 tablespoons tomato chutney
1 tablespoon soft brown sugar
2 teaspoons Worcestershire sauce
1 teaspoon finely chopped
   oregano
1 teaspoon mustard powder

▶

► **MEATLOAF**

800 g (1 lb 12 oz) minced (ground) beef
1 small carrot, diced
1 small celery stalk, diced
1 small red or green capsicum (pepper), seeded and diced
80 g (2³⁄₄ oz/½ cup) fresh or frozen peas

4 spring onions (scallions), chopped
1 tablespoon finely chopped flat-leaf (Italian) parsley
1 teaspoon chopped oregano
1 slice wholegrain bread, crusts removed, finely diced
1 egg, lightly beaten

- To make the tomato chutney sauce, combine the tomatoes, tomato sauce, chutney, brown sugar, Worcestershire sauce, oregano and mustard in a small bowl. Set aside.

- To make the meatloaf, combine the beef, carrot, celery, capsicum, peas, spring onions, parsley, oregano and diced bread. Season well with salt and freshly ground black pepper. Using clean hands, thoroughly combine the mixture. Add a quarter of the tomato sauce to the beef mixture along with the beaten egg and thoroughly mix again. Add 60 ml (2 fl oz /¼ cup) water to the remaining tomato sauce.

- Spray the steaming basket of a 6 litre (210 fl oz) pressure cooker with oil, to grease. Press the beef mixture into the basket. Pour about 1 tablespoon of the tomato sauce over the meatloaf and then spread the remaining sauce over the base of the pressure cooker. Place the basket into the cooker.

- Lock the lid in place and bring the cooker to high pressure over high heat. Once high pressure is reached, reduce the heat to stabilise the pressure and cook for 15 minutes. Remove the cooker from the heat and release the pressure using the natural release method. Remove the lid carefully.

- Turn the meatloaf out onto a board. Cut into wedges and serve with the tomato chutneysauce, and mashed sweet potato and a green salad if desired.

*Beef & veal*

# SMOKED PAPRIKA VEAL WITH ROASTED CAPSICUM

**preparation time:** 15 minutes
**cooking time:** 40 minutes
**serves:** 4

1 kg (2 lb 4 oz) boneless veal
    shoulder
3 teaspoons smoked paprika
60 ml (2 fl oz/¼ cup olive oil
1 onion, sliced
2 garlic cloves, crushed
125 ml (4 fl oz/½ cup) red wine
600 g (1 lb 5 oz) tomato passata
    (puréed tomatoes)

150 ml (5 fl oz) chicken stock
2 all-purpose potatoes, peeled and
    diced
½ teaspoon caraway seeds
2 bay leaves
275 g (9¾ oz) jar roasted red
    capsicums (peppers), drained
    and rinsed
sour cream, to serve

• Cut the veal into 3 cm (1¼ inch) cubes and toss with the paprika and a little salt and freshly ground black pepper.

• Heat half the oil in an 8 litre (280 fl oz) pressure cooker over medium heat and cook the onion and garlic for 3 minutes or until starting to soften. Remove from the cooker and set aside.

• Add the remaining oil to the cooker and heat over high heat. Cook the veal in batches until well browned. Remove from the cooker and set aside.

• Add the wine to the cooker and simmer for 2 minutes, scraping the base of the pot. Return the veal and the onion to the cooker with the tomato passata, stock, potato, caraway seeds and bay leaves and stir well. Lock the lid in place and bring to low pressure over high heat. Once low pressure is reached, reduce the heat to stabilise the pressure and cook for 25 minutes or until the veal is tender.

▶

*Beef & veal*

► ● Remove the cooker from the heat and release the pressure using the natural release method. Remove the lid carefully. Stir through the capsicum. Taste and season with salt and freshly ground black pepper. Serve with a dollop of sour cream and with cooked fettuccine.

# CURRIED SAUSAGES WITH POTATOES AND PEAS

**preparation time:** 15 minutes
**cooking time:** 15–20 minutes
**serves:** 4

1 tablespoon dried red lentils
1 teaspoon black peppercorns
1 small dried red chilli, roughly
   chopped
1/2 teaspoon cumin seeds
1/2 teaspoon coriander seeds
500 g (1 lb 2 oz) beef sausages
3 all-purpose potatoes, cut into
   3 cm (1¼ inch) pieces
1 onion, thickly sliced

2 sprigs curry leaves (optional)
2 tablespoons brandy
100 ml (3½ fl oz) beef stock
1 tablespoon dijon mustard
100 ml (3½ fl oz) pouring cream
155 g (5½ oz/1 cup) frozen peas
1 handful flat-leaf (Italian) parsley,
   chopped

● Using a mortar and pestle or spice grinder, pound or grind the lentils, peppercorns, chilli, cumin seeds and coriander seeds to a fine powder. Push the powder through a fine sieve and set aside.

● Prick the sausages all over. Cook the sausages, uncovered, in a 6 litre (210 fl oz) pressure cooker over medium–high heat until browned all over. Remove the sausages from the cooker and set aside.

- Put the potato and onion over the base of the cooker and top with the sausages and curry leaves, if using. Combine the spice mixture, brandy, stock, mustard and half the cream and pour over the sausages. Lock the lid in place and bring the cooker to high pressure over high heat. Once high pressure is reached, reduce the heat to stabilise the pressure and cook for 7 minutes.

- Remove the cooker from the heat and release the pressure using the natural release method. Remove the lid carefully.

- Stir in the remaining cream and the peas and bring to a simmer over medium heat. Remove the cooker from the heat, cover, and stand for 3–5 minutes or until the peas are bright green and tender.

- Season to taste with salt and freshly ground black pepper. Stir through the parsley and serve with jasmine rice.

# COUNTRY BEEF STEW

**preparation time:** 20 minutes
**cooking time:** 50 minutes
**serves:** 6–8

1 kg (2 lb 4 oz) chuck steak
1 tablespoon olive oil
2 red onions, sliced
2 celery stalks, sliced
3 carrots, chopped
2 garlic cloves, crushed
1 teaspoon ground coriander
1/2 teaspoon allspice
3/4 teaspoon sweet paprika
6 ripe tomatoes, chopped

250 ml (9 fl oz/1 cup) red wine
500 ml (17 fl oz/2 cups) beef stock
2 tablespoons tomato paste
   (concentrated purée)
2 bay leaves
250 g (9 oz) small new potatoes,
   halved
1/4 cup flat-leaf (Italian)
   parsley, chopped

▶

► • Trim the beef and cut into 4 cm (1 1/2 inch) cubes. Heat the oil in a 6 litre (210 fl oz) pressure cooker over medium–high heat and cook the beef in batches until well browned. Remove from the cooker and set aside.

• Add the onion to the cooker and cook over medium heat for 5 minutes or until starting to soften. Add the celery, carrot, garlic, coriander, allspice and paprika. Cook for a further 3 minutes or until aromatic.

• Return the beef to the cooker with the tomato, wine, stock, tomato paste and bay leaves. Bring to a simmer over high heat. Lock the lid in place and bring the cooker to high pressure over high heat. Once high pressure is reached, reduce the heat to stabilise the pressure and cook for 15 minutes.

• Remove the cooker from the heat and release the pressure using the quick release method. Remove the lid carefully.

• Add the potato to the cooker, replace the lid immediately and lock in place. Bring the cooker back to high pressure over high heat, scraping the base of the pot. Once high pressure is reached, reduce the heat to stabilise the pressure and cook for a further 10 minutes or until the beef and potatoes are tender.

• Remove the cooker from the heat and release the pressure using the natural release method. Remove the lid carefully. Season to taste with salt and freshly ground black pepper. Stir through the parsley and serve.

# BEEF CARBONNADE

**preparation time:** 15 minutes
**cooking time:** 50 minutes
**serves:** 4

1.2 kg (2 lb 10 oz) chuck steak
2 tablespoons olive oil
3 onions, chopped
2 garlic cloves, crushed
375 ml (13 fl oz/1½ cups) beer
   (bitter or stout)

1 teaspoon soft brown sugar
2 bay leaves
4 thyme sprigs
1 handful flat-leaf (Italian) parsley,
   chopped

• Trim the beef of excess fat, cut into 4 cm (1½ inch) cubes and season with salt and freshly ground black pepper.

• Heat half the oil in a 6 litre (210 fl oz) pressure cooker over medium heat and cook the onion for 5 minutes or until starting to soften. Add the garlic and cook for a further 2 minutes or until aromatic. Remove from the cooker and set aside.

• Heat the remaining oil in the cooker over high heat and cook the beef in batches until well browned. Return all the beef to the cooker with the onion mixture, beer, brown sugar, bay leaves and thyme and stir well. Season with salt and freshly ground black pepper. Lock the lid in place and bring the cooker to high pressure over high heat. Once high pressure is reached, reduce the heat to stabilise the pressure and cook for 30 minutes or until the beef is tender.

• Remove the cooker from the heat and release the pressure using the natural release method. Remove the lid carefully.

• Season to taste with salt and extra pepper if desired, and sprinkle with the parsley. Serve with green beans or zucchini.

*Beef & veal*

# CORNED BEEF WITH CABBAGE AND POTATOES

**preparation time:** 25 minutes
**cooking time:** 1 hour 10 minutes
**serves:** 6

1 small onion
8 whole cloves
1 tablespoon malt vinegar
1 tablespoon soft brown sugar
8 black peppercorns
2 bay leaves
1.5 kg (3 lb 5 oz) piece corned beef
    (silverside)
12 small new potatoes, halved if large
500 g (1 lb 2 oz) savoy cabbage, core
    attached and cut into 4–6 wedges

**MUSTARD AND PARSLEY SAUCE**
1 egg
2 tablespoons caster (superfine) sugar
1 tablespoon plain (all-purpose) flour
1 teaspoon mustard powder
60 ml (2 fl oz/$^1$/$_4$ cup) malt vinegar
2 tablespoons finely chopped flat-leaf
    (Italian) parsley

● Peel the onion and stud it with the cloves. Put the onion in an 8 litre (280 fl oz) pressure cooker with 500 ml (17 fl oz/2 cups) water, the vinegar, brown sugar, peppercorns and bay leaves and stir until the sugar dissolves.

● Rinse the corned beef, pat dry with paper towel and then trim off any excess fat. Place the beef in the steaming basket or on a trivet in the pressure cooker. Lock the lid in place and bring the cooker to low pressure over high heat. Once low pressure is reached, reduce the heat to stabilise the pressure and cook for 1 hour or until the meat is tender when tested with a skewer.

● Remove the cooker from the heat and release the pressure using the natural release method. Remove the lid carefully. Remove the steaming basket or trivet from the cooker. Transfer the meat to a warm platter and set aside in a warm place to rest.

*Beef & veal*

- Add the potatoes and cabbage to the cooker. Lock the lid in place and bring the cooker to high pressure over high heat. Once high pressure is reached, reduce the heat to stabilise the pressure and cook for a further 5 minutes or until the potatoes are tender.

- Remove the cooker from the heat again and release the pressure using the natural release method. Remove the lid carefully.

- To make the mustard and parsley sauce, remove 250 ml (9 fl oz/1 cup) of the cooking liquid from the cooker and set aside. Whisk together the egg and sugar in a small bowl, then whisk in the flour and mustard powder. Gradually add the reserved cooking liquid and the vinegar, mixing until smooth. Pour into a small saucepan and stir over medium heat until thickened. Stir through the parsley and season with freshly ground black pepper.

- To serve, cut the corned beef into thick slices. Use a slotted spoon to lift the potatoes and cabbage out of the cooker to the serving plates. Discard the onion. Serve with the mustard and parsley sauce, and with some steamed carrots and green beans if desired.

*Note Store leftover corned beef in a bowl with the remaining cooking liquid to cover. Cover with plastic wrap and refrigerate.*

*Beef & veal*

# STIFATHO

**preparation time:** 15 minutes
**cooking time:** 50 minutes
**serves:** 4

1 kg (2 lb 4 oz) chuck steak
1 tablespoon olive oil
500 g (1 lb 2 oz) whole baby
   onions
1 garlic clove, crushed
1 cinnamon stick
4 whole cloves

2 bay leaves
125 ml (4 fl oz/$\frac{1}{2}$ cup) red wine
500 ml (17 fl oz/2 cups) beef stock
1 tablespoon red wine vinegar
2 tablespoons tomato paste
   (concentrated purée)
2 tablespoons currants

• Trim the beef of excess fat, then cut into 5 cm (2 inch) cubes. Heat the oil in a 6 litre (210 fl oz) pressure cooker over medium–high heat and cook the beef in batches until well browned. Remove from the cooker and set aside.

• Add the onions to the cooker and cook over medium–high heat for 5 minutes or until starting to brown. Add the garlic, cinnamon, cloves and bay leaves and cook for 1 minute or until aromatic. Add the wine and simmer for 2 minutes, scraping the base of the pot.

• Return the beef to the cooker with the stock, vinegar and tomato paste. Season with freshly ground black pepper and stir to combine. Lock the lid in place and bring the cooker to high pressure over high heat. Once high pressure is reached, reduce the heat to stabilise the pressure and cook for 25 minutes or until the beef is tender.

• Remove the cooker from the heat and release the pressure using the natural release method. Remove the lid carefully.

• Stir through the currants and simmer, uncovered, for a further 5 minutes or until the currants are plump and the sauce has reduced slightly. Discard the cinnamon stick and season to taste with salt and extra pepper. Serve with rice, bread or potatoes.

# BRAISED VEAL WITH LEMON THYME

preparation time: 10 minutes
cooking time: 55 minutes
serves: 6

2 tablespoons olive oil
1.5 kg (3 lb 5 oz) rack of veal (with
   6 cutlets)
2 leeks, white part only, thinly sliced
30 g (1 oz) butter

1 tablespoon finely grated lemon zest
125 ml (4 fl oz/$^1$/$_2$ cup) chicken stock
125 ml (4 fl oz/$^1$/$_2$ cup) dry white wine
1 tablespoon lemon thyme
125 ml (4 fl oz/$^1$/$_2$ cup) pouring cream

• Heat the oil in a 6 litre (210 fl oz) pressure cooker over medium–high heat and brown the veal well on all sides. Remove the veal from the cooker and set aside.

• Add the leek and butter to the cooker, reduce the heat to medium and cook, stirring occasionally, for 10 minutes or until soft. Add the lemon zest and season with freshly ground black pepper. Stir in the stock and wine and bring to the boil over high heat.

• Return the veal to the cooker. Lock the lid in place and bring the cooker to low pressure over high heat. Once low pressure is reached, reduce the heat to stabilise the pressure and cook for 18–20 minutes or until the veal is tender.

• Remove the cooker from the heat and release the pressure using the natural release method. Remove the lid carefully.

• Remove the veal to a plate, cover and set aside. Add the lemon thyme and cream to the cooker and simmer, uncovered, for a further 10 minutes or until the sauce has reduced slightly.

• Season to taste with salt and freshly ground black pepper. Serve the veal with the sauce and with boiled baby potatoes.

*Beef & veal*

# BEEF OSSO BUCCO

**preparation time:** 15 minutes
**cooking time:** 55 minutes
**serves:** 4

2 tablespoons olive oil
1 onion, finely chopped
1 carrot, finely chopped
2 garlic cloves, crushed
2 bay leaves
1 kg (2 lb 4 oz) beef osso bucco
185 ml (6 fl oz/$^3$/4 cup) white wine
250 ml (9 fl oz /1 cup) beef stock
1 x 400 g (14 oz) tin chopped
    tomatoes

$^1$/2 teaspoon black peppercorns
155 g (5$^1$/2 oz/1 cup) frozen peas
1 handful flat-leaf (Italian) parsley,
    chopped

## GREMOLATA
2 garlic cloves, finely chopped
1 handful flat-leaf (Italian) parsley,
    chopped
finely grated zest of 2 lemons

● Heat half the oil in a 6 litre (210 fl oz) pressure cooker over medium heat and cook the onion and carrot for 10 minutes or until the onion softens. Add the garlic and bay leaves and cook for a further 2 minutes or until aromatic. Remove from the cooker and set aside.

● Season the osso bucco well with salt and freshly ground black pepper. Heat the remaining oil in the cooker over high heat and cook the osso bucco in batches until well browned on all sides. Remove from the cooker and set aside.

● Add half the wine to the cooker and simmer for 2 minutes, scraping the base of the pot. Return the osso bucco to the cooker with the remaining wine, stock, onion mixture, tomatoes and peppercorns and stir well. Lock the lid in place and bring the cooker to high pressure over high heat. Once high pressure is reached, reduce the heat to stabilise the pressure and cook for 25 minutes or until the meat is very tender.

- Meanwhile, make the gremolata. Combine the garlic, parsley and lemon zest in a bowl, cover and set aside.

- Remove the cooker from the heat and release the pressure using the natural release method. Remove the lid carefully. Add the peas and simmer, uncovered, for a further 3 minutes or until the peas are just tender.

- Before serving, season with salt and freshly ground black pepper and stir through the parsley. Transfer to serving plates, sprinkle with the gremolata and serve with mashed potatoes and steamed vegetables.

# VEAL, LEMON AND CAPER CASSEROLE

**preparation time:** 15 minutes
**cooking time:** 1 hour 5 minutes
**serves:** 4

2 tablespoons olive oil
3 leeks, white part only, cut into
    large chunks
2 garlic cloves, crushed
2 bay leaves
300 g (10$^1$/$_2$ oz) French shallots,
    unpeeled
1 kg (2 lb 4 oz) boneless veal
    shoulder

500 ml (17 fl oz/2 cups) chicken
    stock
1 teaspoon finely grated lemon zest
80 ml (2$^1$/$_2$ fl oz/$^1$/$_3$ cup) lemon juice
2 tablespoons capers, rinsed well
chopped flat-leaf (Italian) parsley,
    to serve
caperberries, to garnish (optional)

- Heat half the oil in a 6 litre (210 fl oz) pressure cooker over medium heat and cook the leek for 10 minutes or until softened. Add the garlic and bay leaves and cook for a further 2 minutes or until aromatic. Remove from the cooker and set aside.

▶ • Put the shallots in a heatproof bowl. Pour over boiling water to cover and set aside for 5 minutes to soften. Drain and peel.

• Trim the veal, cut into 4 cm (1 1/2 inch) cubes and season with salt and freshly ground black pepper.

• Heat the remaining oil in the cooker over high heat and cook the shallots for 5 minutes or until golden brown. Remove from the cooker and set aside. Cook the veal in batches over high heat until well browned.

• Return all the veal to the cooker with the leek mixture, shallots, stock, lemon zest and lemon juice and stir well. Lock the lid in place and bring the cooker to low pressure over high heat. Once low pressure is reached, reduce the heat to stabilise the pressure and cook for 25 minutes or until the veal is tender.

• Remove the cooker from the heat and release the pressure using the natural release method. Remove the lid carefully.

• To serve, stir in the capers and season with salt and freshly ground black pepper. Sprinkle with the parsley and garnish with caperberries if desired.

# PORTUGUESE BEEF

**preparation time:** 15 minutes
**cooking time:** 50 minutes
**serves:** 6

1.25 kg (2 lb 12 oz) chuck steak
2 tablespoons olive oil
175 g (6 oz) smoked bacon slices,
    chopped
2 garlic cloves, thinly sliced
1 tablespoon sweet paprika
3/4 teaspoon smoked paprika

2 bay leaves
2 teaspoons dried oregano
250 ml (9 fl oz/1 cup) red wine
250 ml (9 fl oz/1 cup) beef stock
175 g (6 oz/1 cup) green olives
30 g (1 oz/1/4 cup) slivered almonds,
    lightly toasted

• Trim the beef, cut into 4 cm (1 1/2 inch) cubes and season with salt and freshly ground black pepper.

• Heat half the oil in a 8 litre (210 fl oz) pressure cooker over medium–high heat and cook the bacon for 5 minutes or until crisp. Add the garlic, sweet and smoked paprika, bay leaves and oregano and cook for 2 minutes or until aromatic. Remove from the cooker. Heat the remaining oil in the cooker over high heat and cook the beef in batches until well browned on all sides. Remove from the cooker and set aside.

• Add the wine to the cooker and simmer for 2 minutes, scraping the base of the pot. Return the beef to the cooker with the bacon mixture and stock and stir well. Lock the lid in place and bring the cooker to high pressure over high heat. Once high pressure is reached, reduce the heat to stabilise the pressure and cook for 25 minutes or until the meat is tender. Remove the cooker from the heat and release the pressure using the natural release method. Remove the lid carefully.

• Cook over medium heat, uncovered, until the sauce has thickened slightly. Stir through the olives and almonds and season with salt and freshly ground black pepper. Serve with mashed potato or steamed rice.

*Beef & veal*

# BEEF WITH ROOT VEGETABLES AND BROAD BEANS

**preparation time:** 20 minutes
**cooking time:** 50 minutes
**serves:** 4

1.2 kg (2 lb 10 oz) chuck steak
2 tablespoons olive oil
1 leek, white part only, cut into 1 cm
($1/2$ inch) thick slices
1 celery stalk, sliced
2 garlic cloves, chopped
$1/2$ teaspoon dried thyme
250 ml (9 fl oz/1 cup) red wine
125 ml (4 fl oz/$1/2$ cup) beef stock

60 ml (2 fl oz/$1/4$ cup) tomato sauce
(ketchup)
2 parsnips, quartered
300 g (10$1/2$ oz) orange sweet potato,
cut into 8 wedges
1 swede (rutabaga), cut into 8 wedges
175 g (6 oz) frozen broad (fava)
beans

• Trim the beef, cut into 4 cm (1 $1/2$ inch) cubes and season with salt and freshly ground black pepper.

• Heat half the oil in a 6 litre (210 fl oz) pressure cooker over medium heat and cook the leek and celery for 5 minutes or until starting to soften. Add the garlic and thyme and cook for a further 2 minutes or until aromatic. Remove from the cooker and set aside.

• Heat the remaining oil in the cooker over high heat and cook the beef in batches until well browned. Remove from the cooker and set aside. Add the wine and simmer for 2 minutes, scraping the base of the pot.

• Return the beef to the cooker with the leek mixture, stock, 125 ml (4 fl oz/$1/2$ cup) water and the tomato sauce. Lock the lid in place and bring the cooker to high pressure over high heat. Once high pressure is reached, reduce the heat to stabilise

*Beef & veal*

the pressure and cook for 15 minutes. Remove the cooker from the heat and release the pressure using the quick release method. Remove the lid carefully.

• Add the parsnip, orange sweet potato and swede and stir to combine. Replace the lid immediately and lock in place. Bring the cooker back to high pressure over high heat. Once high pressure is reached, reduce the heat to stabilise the pressure and cook for a further 10 minutes.

• Remove the cooker from the heat and release the pressure using the natural release method. Remove the lid carefully.

• Add the broad beans to the cooker and cook, uncovered, over medium heat, stirring occasionally, until the broad beans are tender, then serve.

# BRAISED VEAL SHANKS

**preparation time:** 15 minutes
**cooking time: 55 minutes**
serves: 4–6

2 tablespoons olive oil
1 leek, white part only, finely diced
1 onion, finely diced
1 carrot, finely diced
1 celery stalk, finely diced
2 garlic cloves, finely chopped
1 bay leaf
1 rosemary sprig, leaves chopped
4–6 veal shanks (about 2 kg/4 lb 8 oz)
125 ml (4 fl oz/1/2 cup) red wine

500 ml (17 fl oz/2 cups) veal stock
200 g (7 oz) artichoke halves
80 g (2³/4 oz/1/2 cup) frozen peas

## ORANGE GREMOLATA
1 garlic clove, finely chopped
finely grated zest of 1 orange
1 small handful flat-leaf (Italian)
    parsley leaves, finely chopped

▶

► ● Heat half the oil in a 6 litre (210 fl oz) pressure cooker over medium heat and cook the leek, onion, carrot and celery for 10 minutes or until the leek and onion are softened. Add the garlic, bay leaf and rosemary and cook for a further 2 minutes or until aromatic. Remove from the cooker and set aside.

● Season the shanks well with salt and freshly ground black pepper. Heat the remaining oil in the cooker over high heat and cook the shanks in batches until well browned. Remove from the cooker and set aside.

● Add the wine to the cooker and simmer for 2 minutes, scraping the base of the pot. Return the shanks to the cooker with the leek mixture and stock and stir well. Lock the lid in place and bring the cooker to high pressure over high heat. Once high pressure is reached, reduce the heat to stabilise the pressure and cook for 25 minutes or until the veal is very tender and almost falling off the bone.

● Meanwhile, to make the orange gremolata, combine the garlic, orange zest and parsley in a bowl. Cover and set aside.

● Remove the cooker from the heat and release the pressure using the natural release method. Remove the lid carefully.

● Add the artichokes and peas to the cooker and simmer, uncovered, for 3 minutes or until the peas are just tender. Season to taste with salt and freshly ground black pepper. Serve the veal shanks sprinkled with the gremolata.

*Beef & veal*

# BEEF CHEEKS WITH ONIONS, MUSHROOMS AND THYME

preparation time: 25 minutes
cooking time: 1 hour 20 minutes
serves: 4

1 kg (2 lb 4 oz) beef cheeks
2 tablespoons olive oil
100 g (3½ oz) bacon or speck,
    trimmed of fat, chopped
1 onion, finely chopped
2 celery stalks, finely chopped
1 carrot, finely chopped
3 garlic cloves, crushed
4 thyme sprigs

250 ml (9 fl oz/1 cup) red wine
400 ml (14 fl oz) beef stock
2 bay leaves
40 g (1½ oz) butter
12 baby onions, peeled and trimmed,
    halved lengthways if large
1½ tablespoons sugar
1½ tablespoons sherry vinegar
16 button mushrooms, halved

• Trim the beef cheeks of excess fat and sinew, then cut each into four portions.
Season with salt and freshly ground black pepper.

• Heat half the oil in a 6 litre (210 fl oz) pressure cooker over medium–high heat
and cook the bacon for 5 minutes or until crisp. Remove from the cooker and set
aside. Add the onion, celery and carrot to the cooker and cook over medium heat
for 10 minutes or until softened. Add the garlic and thyme and cook for a further
2 minutes or until aromatic. Remove from the cooker and set aside.

• Heat the remaining oil in the cooker over high heat and cook the beef in batches
until well browned. Remove from the cooker and set aside.

• Add the wine to the cooker and simmer for 2 minutes, scraping the base of the pot.
Return the beef to the cooker with the bacon, onion mixture, stock, 400 ml (14 fl oz)
water and the bay leaves. Lock the lid in place and bring the cooker to high pressure

▶

*Beef & veal*

▶ over high heat. Once high pressure is reached, reduce the heat to stabilise the pressure and cook for 45 minutes or until the meat is almost falling apart.

● Meanwhile, place half of the butter in a heavy-based frying pan, add the baby onions and cook over low–medium heat for about 8 minutes, or until golden. Add the sugar and cook until caramelised, shaking the pan occasionally to ensure that it caramelises evenly. Add half the vinegar and stir to remove any sediment from the bottom of the pan. Remove from the pan and set aside.

● Melt the remaining butter in the pan and cook the mushrooms over medium heat for 5–6 minutes, or until golden. Pour in the remaining vinegar and stir to remove any sediment from the bottom of the pan. Set aside.

● Remove the cooker from the heat and release the pressure using the natural release method. Remove the lid carefully.

● Add the caramelised onions to the cooker, replace the lid immediately and lock in place. Bring the cooker back to high pressure over high heat. Once high pressure is reached, reduce the heat to stabilise the pressure and cook for a further 5 minutes.

● Remove the cooker from the heat and release the pressure using the natural release method. Remove the lid carefully. Stir through the mushrooms.

● Serve the beef cheeks with the sauce, and with mashed potato and steamed green vegetables if desired.

# MUSSAMAN CURRY

preparation time: 15 minutes
cooking time: 40 minutes
serves: 4

800 g (1 lb 12 oz) chuck steak
1 tablespoon peanut oil
2 tablespoons mussaman curry paste
2 cm ($3/4$ inch) piece ginger, shredded
2 cinnamon sticks
10 cardamom seeds
5 cloves
1 x 400 ml (14 fl oz) tin coconut milk
100 ml ($3^{1}/2$ fl oz) beef stock

1 tablespoon tamarind purée
2–3 all-purpose potatoes, peeled and
    cut into 1 cm ($1/2$ inch) dice
110 g ($3^{3}/4$ oz/$2/3$ cup) roasted
    salted peanuts, very finely ground
60 ml (2 fl oz/$1/4$ cup) fish sauce
30 g (1 oz/$1/4$ cup) grated palm sugar
    (jaggery) or soft brown sugar

• Trim the beef, cut into 5 cm (2 inch) cubes and season with salt and freshly ground black pepper. Heat the oil in a 6 litre (210 fl oz) pressure cooker over high heat and cook the beef in batches until well browned. Remove from the cooker and set aside.

• Add the curry paste, ginger, cinnamon sticks, cardamom and cloves to the cooker and cook over medium heat for 2 minutes or until aromatic.

• Return the beef to the cooker and stir in 300 ml ($10^{1}/2$ fl oz) of the coconut milk, the stock, tamarind and half the potato. Lock the lid in place and bring the cooker to high pressure over high heat. Once high pressure is reached, reduce the heat to stabilise the pressure and cook for 15 minutes.

• Remove the cooker from the heat and release the pressure using the quick release method. Remove the lid carefully.

• Stir in the remaining coconut milk, remaining potato, three-quarters of the ground peanuts, the fish sauce and palm sugar. Replace the lid immediately and lock in place. ▶

*Beef & veal*

▶ Bring the cooker back to high pressure over high heat. Once high pressure is reached, reduce the heat to stabilise the pressure and cook for a further 10 minutes or until the beef and potatoes are tender.

● Remove the cooker from the heat again and release the pressure using the quick release method. Remove the lid carefully. Stir through the remaining ground peanuts.

● Taste, then adjust the seasoning with salt and freshly ground black pepper if necessary. Spoon into serving bowls and serve with steamed rice.

# OXTAIL WITH MARMALADE

**preparation time:** 20 minutes (+ overnight marinating)
**cooking time:** 45 minutes
**serves:** 4

1.5 kg (3 lb 5 oz) oxtail
160 g (5$^3$/$_4$ oz/$^1$/$_2$ cup) marmalade
100 ml (3$^1$/$_2$ fl oz) sherry
2 tablespoons olive oil
500 ml (17 fl oz/2 cups) beef stock
4 all-purpose potatoes, cut into
   3 cm (1$^1$/$_4$ inch) pieces

2 carrots, sliced
1 onion, thinly sliced
2 bay leaves
1 cinnamon stick
1 orange, peeled and segmented

● Cut the oxtail into sections, then combine with the marmalade and sherry in a large bowl. Cover and place in the refrigerator to marinate overnight.

● Remove the oxtail from the marinade. Heat the oil in an 8 litre (280 fl oz) pressure cooker over high heat and cook the oxtail in batches for about 4 minutes on each side or until well browned all over.

● Return all the oxtail to the cooker with the stock, potato, carrot, onion, bay leaves and cinnamon stick. Stir well. Lock the lid in place and bring the cooker to high pressure over high heat. Once high pressure is reached, reduce the heat to stabilise the pressure and cook for 30 minutes or until the oxtail is very tender.

● Remove the cooker from the heat and release the pressure using the natural release method. Remove the lid carefully.

● Season with salt and freshly ground black pepper. Top the oxtail with the orange segments and serve with mashed potato.

# Lamb

Prepare these hearty, succulent lamb
curries and stews with little fuss and
no more than a pressure cooker.

# GREEK LAMB WITH MACARONI

preparation time: 15 minutes
cooking time: 40 minutes
serves: 4–6

1 kg (2 lb 4 oz) boneless lamb leg
2 tablespoons olive oil
1 large onion, chopped
2 garlic cloves, crushed
1 teaspoon dried oregano
500 ml (17 fl oz/2 cups) beef stock
1 x 400 g (14 oz) tin chopped
  tomatoes

60 g (2$^1$/$_4$ oz/$^1$/$_4$ cup) tomato paste
  (concentrated purée)
2 tablespoons red wine vinegar
1 tablespoon soft brown sugar
200 g (7 oz/2 cups) macaroni pasta
125 g (4$^1$/$_2$ oz) pecorino cheese,
  grated

● Trim the lamb of excess fat, cut into 3 cm (1 1/4 inch) cubes and season with salt
and freshly ground black pepper.

● Heat half the oil in a 6 litre (210 fl oz) pressure cooker over medium heat and cook
the onion for 5 minutes or until starting to soften. Add the garlic and oregano and
cook for a further 2 minutes or until aromatic. Remove from the cooker and set aside.

● Heat the remaining oil in the cooker over high heat and cook the lamb in batches
until well browned.

● Return all the lamb to the cooker with the onion mixture, stock, tomatoes, tomato
paste, vinegar and brown sugar and stir well, scraping the base of the pot. Lock the
lid in place and bring the cooker to low pressure over high heat. Once low pressure
is reached, reduce the heat to stabilise the pressure and cook for 20 minutes or until
the meat is tender.

● Meanwhile, cook the macaroni following the packet directions until al dente. Drain. ▶

*Lamb*

● Remove the cooker from the heat and release the pressure using the natural release method. Remove the lid carefully. Stir through the drained macaroni. Divide among serving bowls and sprinkle with the cheese.

# BRAISED LAMB WITH CAPSICUM AND FENNEL

**preparation time:** 15 minutes
**cooking time:** 40 minutes
**serves:** 4

1 kg (2 lb 4 oz) lamb shoulder
1 tablespoon olive oil
1 large onion, chopped
1 red capsicum (pepper), seeded and
    sliced into strips
1 yellow capsicum (pepper), seeded
    and sliced into strips
2 fennel bulbs, trimmed and each cut
    into thick slices lengthways

4 garlic cloves, chopped
100 ml (3$^1$/2 fl oz) beef stock or water
250 g (9 oz/1 cup) tomato passata
    (puréed tomatoes)
1 tablespoon tomato paste
    (concentrated purée)
2 teaspoons Worcestershire sauce
fennel fronds, to garnish

● Trim the lamb of excess fat and cut into 4 cm (1 $^1$/2 inch) cubes. Heat the oil in a 6 litre (210 fl oz) pressure cooker over medium–high heat and cook the lamb in batches until well browned. Remove from the cooker and set aside.

● Add the onion to the cooker and cook over medium heat for 5 minutes or until starting to soften. Add the red and yellow capsicum, fennel and garlic and cook for a further 3 minutes or until aromatic.

Lamb

- Return the lamb to the cooker with the stock, tomato passata, tomato paste and Worcestershire sauce. Season with salt and freshly ground black pepper. Stir well. Lock the lid in place and bring the cooker to high pressure over high heat. Once high pressure is reached, reduce the heat to stabilise the pressure and cook for 20 minutes or until the lamb is very tender.

- Remove the cooker from the heat and release the pressure using the natural release method. Remove the lid carefully.

- To serve, divide the lamb among the serving bowls and scatter over some chopped fennel fronds.

# LAMB CHOPS IN RATATOUILLE

**preparation time:** 20 minutes
**cooking time:** 25 minutes
**serves:** 6

1 kg (2 lb 4 oz) lamb forequarter chops
1 tablespoon olive oil
1 red onion, cut into 1 cm (1/2 inch) pieces
1 eggplant (aubergine), cut into 2 cm (3/4 inch) cubes
1 red capsicum (pepper), seeded and cut into 2 cm (3/4 inch) cubes
1 green capsicum (pepper), seeded and cut into 2 cm (3/4 inch) cubes
2 garlic cloves, chopped
60 ml (2 fl oz/1/4 cup) chicken stock

1 x 400 g (14 oz) tin chopped tomatoes
2 tablespoons tomato paste (concentrated purée)
2 tablespoons rinsed capers
4 anchovies, chopped
80 g (2 3/4 oz/1/2 cup) pitted kalamata olives, chopped
1 small handful flat-leaf (Italian) parsley leaves, chopped
150 g (5 1/2 oz/3/4 cup) Israeli couscous (see Note), cooked, to serve (optional)

Lamb

▶

▶ • Trim the lamb chops of excess fat and season with salt and freshly ground black pepper. Heat the oil in an 8 litre (280 fl oz) pressure cooker over medium–high heat and cook the chops in batches until browned. Remove from the cooker and set aside.

• Add the onion, eggplant, red and green capsicum and garlic to the cooker and cook over medium heat for 2–3 minutes or until aromatic.

• Return the chops to the pressure cooker with the stock, tomatoes, tomato paste, capers, anchovies, olives and half the parsley. Lock the lid in place and bring the cooker to high pressure over high heat. Once high pressure is reached, reduce the heat to stabilise the pressure and cook for 10 minutes or until the chops are tender.

• Remove the cooker from the heat and release the pressure using the natural release method. Remove the lid carefully.

• Season with salt and freshly ground black pepper, and sprinkle with the remaining parsley. Serve with the couscous if desired.

*note Israeli couscous is larger in size than the more familiar Moroccan couscous, and has a chewier texture. It is sold in most gourmet food stores and health food stores.*

# NAVARIN OF LAMB

preparation time: 20 minutes
cooking time: 55 minutes
serves: 4

1 kg (2 lb 4 oz) boneless lean lamb
   shoulder
2–3 tablespoons olive oil
1 onion, chopped
1 garlic clove, crushed
1 large rosemary sprig
2 thyme sprigs
1 bay leaf
8 bulb spring onions (scallions)
200 g (7 oz) baby turnips
300 g (10$^1/_2$ oz) new potatoes,
   peeled (halved if large)

125 ml (4 fl oz/$^1/_2$ cup) red wine
375 ml (13 fl oz/1$^1/_2$ cups) chicken
   stock
2 tablespoons tomato paste
   (concentrated purée)
18 baby carrots
155 g (5$^1/_2$ oz/1 cup) fresh or frozen
   peas
1 handful flat-leaf (Italian) parsley,
   chopped

• Trim the lamb of excess fat, cut into 2 cm (3/4 inch) cubes and season with salt and freshly ground black pepper.

• Heat half the oil in a 6 litre (210 fl oz) pressure cooker over medium heat and cook the onion for 5 minutes or until starting to soften. Add the garlic, rosemary, thyme and bay leaf and cook for a further 2 minutes or until aromatic. Remove from the cooker and set aside.

• Trim the spring onions. Heat 1 tablespoon of the remaining oil in the cooker over medium–high heat and cook the spring onions, turnips and potatoes in batches until lightly browned. Remove from the cooker and set aside in separate bowls.

• Heat a little more oil if necessary in the cooker over high heat and cook the lamb in batches until well browned. Remove from the cooker and set aside.

▶

▶ • Add the wine to the cooker and simmer for 2 minutes, scraping the base of the pot. Combine the stock and tomato paste and stir until smooth. Return the lamb to the cooker with the stock mixture and onion mixture. Stir well. Lock the lid in place and bring the cooker to low pressure over high heat. Once low pressure is reached, reduce the heat to stabilise the pressure and cook for 18 minutes.

• Remove the cooker from the heat and release the pressure using the quick release method. Remove the lid carefully. Add the turnips and potatoes and stir to distribute evenly. Replace the lid immediately and lock in place. Bring the cooker back to low pressure over high heat. Once low pressure is reached, reduce the heat to stabilise the pressure and cook for a further 6 minutes.

• Meanwhile, trim the carrots, leaving a little bit of green stalk.

• Remove the cooker from the heat and release the pressure using the quick release method. Remove the lid carefully. Stir through the spring onions and carrots. Replace the lid immediately and lock in place. Bring the cooker back to low pressure over high heat. Once low pressure is reached, reduce the heat to stabilise the pressure and cook for a further 3 minutes or until the lamb and vegetables are tender.

• Remove the cooker from the heat and release the pressure using the natural release method. Remove the lid carefully.

• Stir through the peas and parsley and cook, uncovered, over medium heat for a further 3 minutes, or until the peas are tender. Season with salt and freshly ground black pepper before serving.

*Lamb*

# MOROCCAN SPICED LAMB WITH PUMPKIN

preparation time: 20 minutes
cooking time: 45 minutes
serves: 6

1.5 kg (3 lb 5 oz) boneless lamb
    shoulder
1 tablespoon olive oil
1 large onion, diced
1 teaspoon ground coriander
1/2 teaspoon ground ginger
1/2 teaspoon cayenne pepper
1/4 teaspoon ground saffron threads

1 cinnamon stick
500 ml (17 fl oz/2 cups) chicken stock
500 g (1 lb 2 oz) pumpkin (winter
    squash), cut into 2 cm (3/4 inch)
    pieces
100 g (3 1/2 oz) dried apricots
coriander (cilantro) sprigs, to garnish

- Trim the lamb of excess fat, cut into 3 cm (1 1/4 inch) cubes and season with salt and freshly ground black pepper.

- Heat half the oil in a 6 litre (210 fl oz) pressure cooker over medium heat and cook the onion for 5 minutes or until starting to soften. Add the ground coriander, ginger, cayenne pepper, saffron and cinnamon stick and cook for a further 2 minutes or until aromatic. Remove from the cooker and set aside.

- Heat the remaining oil in the cooker over high heat and cook the lamb in batches until well browned on all sides.

- Return all the lamb to the cooker with the onion mixture and stock and stir well. Lock the lid in place and bring the cooker to high pressure over high heat. Once high pressure is reached, reduce the heat to stabilise the pressure and cook for 15 minutes.

- Remove the cooker from the heat and release the pressure using the quick release method. Remove the lid carefully. Stir in the pumpkin and apricots, replace the lid immediately and lock in place. Bring back to high pressure over high heat. Once high

Lamb

▶ pressure is reached, reduce the heat to stabilise the pressure and cook for 5 minutes or until the lamb and pumpkin are tender.

● Remove the cooker from the heat and release the pressure using the natural release method. Remove the lid carefully.

● Taste the sauce and adjust the seasoning with salt and freshly ground black pepper if necessary. Garnish with the coriander sprigs and serve with couscous or rice.

# LAMB BIRYANI

**preparation time:** 20 minutes (+ overnight marinating)
**cooking time:** 35 minutes
**serves:** 6

1 kg (2 lb 4 oz) boneless lamb
   shoulder
8 cm (3¹/4 inch) piece ginger,
   grated
2 garlic cloves, crushed
2 green chillies, finely chopped
250 g (9 oz/1 cup) Greek-style
   yoghurt
2 tablespoons garam masala
¹/2 teaspoon chilli powder

¹/2 teaspoon ground turmeric
1 tablespoon olive oil
2 onions, thinly sliced
750 ml (26 fl oz/3 cups) chicken stock
¹/2 teaspoon saffron threads
2 tablespoons hot milk
400 g (14 oz/2 cups) basmati rice
40 g (1¹/2 oz) butter, diced
1 handful coriander (cilantro)
   leaves, chopped

● Trim the lamb of excess fat and cut into 3 cm (1¹/4 inch) cubes. Put in a bowl with the ginger, garlic, chilli and yoghurt. Cover and set aside.

● Put the garam masala, chilli powder and turmeric in a small non-stick frying pan and cook over medium heat until aromatic. Add to the lamb mixture, season well with salt and freshly ground black pepper and mix well to coat the lamb in the marinade. Cover and marinate in the refrigerator overnight.

- Heat the oil in a 6 litre (210 fl oz) pressure cooker over medium–high heat and cook the onion for 10 minutes or until lightly golden.

- Add the lamb with the marinade to the cooker with the stock and stir well. Lock the lid in place and bring the cooker to low pressure over high heat. Once low pressure is reached, reduce the heat to stabilise the pressure and cook for 15 minutes.

- Meanwhile, put the saffron in a bowl with the hot milk and set aside for 10 minutes to soak.

- Remove the cooker from the heat and release the pressure using the quick release method. Remove the lid carefully. Stir in the rice, saffron mixture and butter, replace the lid immediately and lock in place. Bring the cooker back to low pressure over high heat. Once low pressure is reached, reduce the heat to stabilise the pressure and cook for 6 minutes or until the lamb and rice are tender.

- Remove the cooker from the heat and release the pressure using the natural release method. Remove the lid carefully. Use a fork to separate the grains. Serve sprinkled with the coriander.

*Lamb*

# CHUTNEY CHOPS WITH POTATOES AND PEAS

**preparation time:** 15 minutes
**cooking time:** 30 minutes
**serves:** 4

1.2 kg (2 lb 10 oz) lamb forequarter
   chops
1 tablespoon olive oil
2 garlic cloves, crushed
2 rosemary sprigs
125 ml (4 fl oz/$1/2$ cup) red wine
1 x 400 g (14 oz) tin chopped
   tomatoes

4 all-purpose potatoes, such as
   desiree, peeled, cut into 4 cm
   ($1^1/2$ inch) chunks
1 x 240 g ($8^1/2$ oz) jar tomato fruit
   chutney
125 ml (4 fl oz/$1/2$ cup) chicken stock
80 g ($2^3/4$ oz/$1/2$ cup) fresh or
   frozen peas

- Trim the lamb chops of excess fat and season with salt and freshly ground black pepper. Heat the oil in an 8 litre (280 fl oz) pressure cooker over medium–high heat and cook the chops in batches until browned. Remove from the cooker and set aside.

- Reduce the heat to medium, add the garlic and rosemary to the cooker and cook for 1 minute or until aromatic. Add the wine and simmer for 2 minutes, scraping the base of the pot. Stir in the tomatoes, potato, chutney and stock, then add the chops.

- Lock the lid in place and bring the cooker to high pressure over high heat. Once high pressure is reached, reduce the heat to stabilise the pressure and cook for 10 minutes or until the chops and potatoes are tender.

- Remove the cooker from the heat and release the pressure using the natural release method. Remove the lid carefully.

- Stir through the peas and cook, uncovered, over medium heat for 3 minutes or until the peas are tender. Season to taste with salt and freshly ground black pepper before serving.

Lamb

# SAAG LAMB

preparation time: 25 minutes (+ overnight marinating)
cooking time: 25 minutes
serves: 4

1 kg (2 lb 4 oz) boneless lamb
   shoulder
1 teaspoon fenugreek seeds
1 teaspoon cumin seeds
1 teaspoon mustard seeds
2 onions, diced
2 garlic cloves, finely chopped
2 teaspoons grated fresh ginger
2 small red chillies, seeded and
   finely diced
2 cinnamon sticks

4 curry leaves
500 ml (17 fl oz/2 cups) beef stock
400 g (14 oz) baby English spinach

## CORIANDER YOGHURT
125 g (4$^1/_2$ oz/$^1/_2$ cup) Greek-style
   yoghurt
1 tablespoon lemon juice
1 small handful coriander (cilantro)
   leaves, chopped

- Trim the lamb of excess fat and cut into 3 cm (1¼ inch) cubes. Put the lamb in a large bowl.

- Using a mortar and pestle or spice grinder, pound or grind the fenugreek, cumin and mustard seeds. Combine the ground spices with the onion, garlic, ginger and chilli. Stir the spice mixture into the bowl with lamb, stirring well to coat the lamb with the spices. Cover and leave to marinate in the refrigerator overnight.

- Put the lamb and marinade, cinnamon sticks, curry leaves and stock in a 6 litre (210 fl oz) pressure cooker and stir well. Lock the lid in place and bring the cooker to high pressure over high heat. Once high pressure is reached, reduce the heat to stabilise the pressure and cook for 20 minutes or until the meat is tender.

- Meanwhile, to make the coriander yoghurt, combine the yoghurt, lemon juice and coriander. Cover and refrigerate.

▶

► ● Remove the cooker from the heat and release the pressure using the natural release method. Remove the lid carefully.

● Stir the spinach through the lamb and set aside until just wilted. Serve with the coriander yoghurt and steamed basmati rice.

# AFRICAN-STYLE LAMB AND PEANUT STEW

**preparation time:** 25 minutes
**cooking time:** 55 minutes
**serves:** 4–6

1 kg (2 lb 4 oz) boneless lamb
   shoulder
2 tablespoons vegetable oil
1 large onion, chopped
1 red capsicum (pepper), seeded
   and chopped
4 garlic cloves, chopped
1 red or green chilli, seeded and
   finely chopped
3 teaspoons curry powder
1 teaspoon dried oregano
2 bay leaves

large pinch cayenne pepper
400 ml (14 fl oz) chicken stock
1 x 400 g (14 oz) tin chopped
   tomatoes
100 ml (3$^{1}/_{2}$ fl oz) tomato sauce
   (ketchup)
90 g (3$^{1}/_{4}$ oz/$^{1}/_{3}$ cup) crunchy or
   smooth peanut butter
1 x 185 ml (6 fl oz) tin coconut milk
1 tablespoon lemon juice
155 g (5$^{1}/_{2}$ oz/1 cup) fresh or frozen
   peas

● Trim the lamb of excess fat, cut into 2 cm (³/4 inch) cubes and season with salt and freshly ground black pepper. Heat half the oil in a 6 litre (210 fl oz) pressure cooker over high heat and cook the lamb in batches until well browned on all sides. Remove from the cooker and set aside.

● Heat the remaining oil in the cooker over medium heat and cook the onion and

*Lamb*

capsicum for 5 minutes or until starting to soften. Add the garlic, chilli, curry powder, oregano, bay leaves and cayenne pepper and cook for 2 minutes or until aromatic.

● Add the stock, tomatoes and tomato sauce to the cooker and bring to a simmer, scraping the base of the pot. Stir in the lamb. Lock the lid in place and bring the cooker to high pressure over high heat. Once high pressure is reached, reduce the heat to stabilise the pressure and cook for 20 minutes or until the lamb is tender.

● Remove the cooker from the heat and release the pressure using the natural release method. Remove the lid carefully.

● Combine the peanut butter, coconut milk and lemon juice in a bowl and stir until smooth. Stir into the stew with the peas. Cook, uncovered, over medium heat until heated through and the peas are tender

● Remove the bay leaves. Divide the stew among bowls and serve with steamed rice or couscous.

Lamb

# HARIRA

**preparation time:** 15 minutes
**cooking time:** 30 minutes
**serves:** 4

600 g (1 lb 5 oz) boneless lamb
   shoulder
2 tablespoons olive oil
1 onion, chopped
2 garlic cloves, crushed
1 teaspoon ground coriander
2 teaspoons ground cumin
2 teaspoons paprika
1/2 teaspoon ground cloves
1/2 teaspoon cayenne pepper

1/2 teaspoon ground cinnamon
1 bay leaf
750 ml (26 fl oz/3 cups) chicken stock
500 g (1 lb 2 oz/2 cups) tomato
   passata (puréed tomatoes)
11/2 x 400 g (14 oz) tins chickpeas,
   drained and rinsed (see Note)
finely grated zest of 1 lemon
2 large handfuls coriander (cilantro)
   leaves, chopped

*Lamb*

● Trim the lamb of excess fat, cut into bite-sized cubes (about 5 mm/1/4 inch) and season with salt and freshly ground black pepper.

● Heat half the oil in a 6 litre (210 fl oz) pressure cooker over medium heat and cook the onion for 5 minutes or until starting to soften. Add the garlic, ground coriander, cumin, paprika, cloves, cayenne pepper, cinnamon and bay leaf and cook for a further 2 minutes or until aromatic. Add the lamb and stir for 2 minutes or until the lamb is coated in the spices.

● Add the stock and tomato passata and bring to a simmer over high heat. Stir well. Lock the lid in place and bring the cooker to high pressure over high heat. Once high pressure is reached, reduce the heat to stabilise the pressure and cook for 15 minutes.

● Remove the cooker from the heat and release the pressure using the natural release method. Stir the chickpeas and lemon zest through the soup and cook over medium heat, uncovered, until heated through. Stir through the coriander and serve.

*Note You can replace the tinned chickpeas with 375 g (13 oz/2¹/4 cups) cooked dried chickpeas (see page 15 for pressure cooking instructions).*

# LAMB SHANKS WITH BARLEY

**preparation time:** 20 minutes (+ overnight soaking)
**cooking time:** 50 minutes
**serves:** 4

165 g (5³/4 oz/³/4 cup) pearl barley
4 Frenched lamb shanks (1.2 kg/
   2 lb 10 oz)
2 tablespoons olive oil
1 onion, chopped
3 garlic cloves, crushed
1 teaspoon dried oregano

125 ml (4 fl oz/¹/2 cup) white wine
   or water
750 ml (26 fl oz/3 cups) chicken stock
2 x 400 g (14 oz) tins chopped
   tomatoes
2 tablespoons tomato paste
   (concentrated purée)
1 rosemary sprig

● Put the barley in a bowl and add plenty of water to cover. Soak for 8 hours or overnight, then drain. Trim the lamb shanks of all fat and season with salt and freshly ground black pepper.

● Heat half the oil in an 8 litre (280 fl oz) pressure cooker over medium heat and cook the onion for 5 minutes or until starting to soften. Add the garlic and oregano and cook for a further 2 minutes or until aromatic. Remove from the cooker and set aside.

● Heat the remaining oil in the cooker over high heat and cook the shanks in batches until well browned on all sides. Remove from the cooker and set aside.

● Add the wine to the cooker and simmer for 2 minutes, scraping the base of the pot. Return the onion to the cooker with the drained barley, stock, tomatoes, tomato paste ▶

*Lamb*

▶ and rosemary sprig. Season with salt and freshly ground black pepper. Bring to a simmer over high heat and stir well. Add the lamb shanks and stir well again.

- Lock the lid in place and bring the cooker to high pressure over high heat. Once high pressure is reached, reduce the heat to stabilise the pressure and cook for 25 minutes or until the lamb and barley are tender.

- Remove the cooker from the heat and release the pressure using the natural release method. Remove the lid carefully.

- Remove the rosemary. Skim off any surface fat before serving with steamed green beans and zucchini (courgettes) if desired.

# IRISH STEW

**preparation time:** 20 minutes
**cooking time:** 40 minutes
**serves:** 6–8

8 lamb neck chops
2 tablespoons olive oil
1 onion, cut into 16 wedges
1 small leek, white part only,
    thickly sliced
4 bacon slices, cut into strips
375 ml (13 fl oz/1¹/₂ cups) beef stock

600 g (1 lb 5 oz) all-purpose
    potatoes, peeled and cut into
    2.5 cm (1 inch) chunks
3 carrots, thickly sliced
150 g (5¹/₂ oz) savoy cabbage,
    thinly sliced
2 tablespoons finely chopped flat-leaf
    (Italian) parsley

- Season the lamb chops with salt and freshly ground black pepper.

- Heat half the oil in an 8 litre (280 fl oz) pressure cooker over medium heat and cook the onion and leek for 10 minutes or until softened. Remove from the cooker and set aside. Add the bacon to the cooker and cook over medium–high heat for 5 minutes or until crisp. Remove from the cooker and set aside.

- Heat the remaining oil in the cooker over high heat and cook the chops in batches until well browned on all sides.

- Return all the chops to the cooker with the onion mixture, bacon, stock, potato and carrot and stir well, scraping the base of the pot. Lock the lid in place and bring the cooker to high pressure over high heat. Once high pressure is reached, reduce the heat to stabilise the pressure and cook for 10 minutes or until the chops are tender.

- Remove the cooker from the heat and release the pressure using the natural release method. Remove the lid carefully.

- Add the cabbage to the cooker. Cook, uncovered, over medium heat, stirring occasionally, for 5 minutes or until the cabbage is tender.

- Taste and check for seasoning. Divide the stew among shallow bowls and sprinkle with the parsley. Serve with bread to mop up the juices.

Lamb

# LAMB WITH GREEN OLIVES AND PRESERVED LEMON

**preparation time:** 20 minutes
**cooking time:** 30 minutes
**serves:** 4

1/2 preserved lemon
1 kg (2 lb 4 oz) lamb forequarter
  chops
2 tablespoons olive oil
1 onion, sliced
2 garlic cloves, crushed
2 cm (3/4 inch) piece ginger,
  finely diced
1 teaspoon ground cumin

1/2 teaspoon ground turmeric
625 ml (21 1/2 fl oz/2 1/2 cups) chicken
  stock
400 g (14 oz) all-purpose potatoes,
  cut into 2.5 cm (1 inch) chunks
2 tablespoons chopped flat-leaf
  (Italian) parsley
2 tablespoons chopped coriander
  (cilantro) leaves

• Rinse the preserved lemon well, remove and discard the pulp and membrane and finely dice the rind. Set aside. Trim the lamb chops of excess fat, then cut each chop in half and season with salt and freshly ground black pepper.

• Heat half the oil in a 6 litre (210 fl oz) pressure cooker over medium heat and cook the onion for 5 minutes or until starting to soften. Add the garlic, ginger, cumin and turmeric and cook for a further 2 minutes or until aromatic. Remove from the cooker and set aside.

• Heat the remaining oil in the cooker over high heat and cook the chops in batches until well browned on both sides.

• Return all the chops to the pressure cooker with the onion mixture, stock, potato and half the combined parsley and coriander leaves. Stir well.

- Lock the lid in place and bring the cooker to high pressure over high heat. Once high pressure is reached, reduce the heat to stabilise the pressure and cook for 10 minutes or until the chops are tender.

- Remove the cooker from the heat and release the pressure using the natural release method. Remove the lid carefully.

- Stir through the remaining parsley and coriander and season to taste with salt and freshly ground black pepper. Serve with rice.

# LAMB MADRAS

**preparation time:** 15 minutes
**cooking time:** 45 minutes
**serves:** 4

1 kg (2 lb 4 oz) boneless lamb
   shoulder
2 tablespoons vegetable oil
1 onion, finely chopped
6 cardamom pods, lightly crushed
4 cloves
2 bay leaves
1 cinnamon stick

60 g (2 1/4 oz/1/4 cup) madras curry
   paste
500 ml (17 fl oz/2 cups) chicken stock
185 g (6 1/2 oz/3/4 cup) Greek-style
   yoghurt
1/4 teaspoon garam masala
2 long red chillies, chopped (optional)

- Trim the lamb of excess fat, cut into 3 cm (1 1/4 inch) cubes and season with salt and freshly ground black pepper. Heat half the oil in a 6 litre (210 fl oz) pressure cooker over high heat and cook the lamb in batches until well browned. Set aside.

▶

● Heat the remaining oil in the cooker over medium heat and cook the onion for 5 minutes or until starting to soften. Add the cardamom pods, cloves, bay leaves and cinnamon stick and cook for 2 minutes. Add the curry paste and cook for 2 minutes or until aromatic. Add the stock and bring to a simmer, scraping the base of the pot.

● Return all the lamb to the cooker and stir well. Lock the lid in place and bring the cooker to high pressure over high heat. Once high pressure is reached, reduce the heat to stabilise the pressure and cook for 20 minutes or until the meat is tender.

● Remove the cooker from the heat and release the pressure using the natural release method. Remove the lid carefully. Stir through the yoghurt and season with salt. Divide among serving bowls and sprinkle with the garam masala and chilli, if desired. Serve with rice.

# ROSEMARY LAMB AND LENTIL CASSEROLE

**preparation time:** 20 minutes
**cooking time:** 55 minutes
**serves:** 4–6

185 g (6$^1/_2$ oz/1 cup) green or brown lentils
1 litre (35 fl oz/4 cups) lamb or chicken stock
1 kg (2 lb 4 oz) boned lamb leg
2 tablespoons olive oil
1 onion, thinly sliced
1 small carrot, finely chopped

2 garlic cloves, crushed
2 teaspoons finely chopped fresh ginger
2 teaspoons rosemary leaves
1 tablespoon soft brown sugar
2 teaspoons balsamic vinegar
rosemary sprigs, to garnish

• Put the lentils in a 6 litre (210 fl oz) pressure cooker with 600 ml (21 fl oz) of the stock and 400 ml (14 fl oz) water. Lock the lid in place and bring the cooker to low pressure over high heat. Once low pressure is reached, reduce the heat to stabilise the pressure and cook for 12 minutes or until the lentils are tender.

• Remove the cooker from the heat and release the pressure using the natural release method. Remove the lid carefully. Drain the lentils, reserving the cooking liquid. Place the lentils in a bowl and set aside. Wash out the pot.

• Trim the lamb of excess fat, cut into 3 cm (1 1/4 inch) cubes and season with salt and freshly ground black pepper.

• Heat half the oil in the cooker over medium heat and cook the onion and carrot for 5 minutes or until starting to soften. Add the garlic, ginger and rosemary and cook for a further 2 minutes or until aromatic. Remove from the cooker and set aside.

• Heat the remaining oil in the cooker over high heat and cook the lamb in batches until well browned.

• Return all the lamb to the cooker with the onion mixture, the remaining stock, brown sugar and vinegar and bring to a simmer. Stir well. Lock the lid in place and bring the cooker to low pressure over high heat. Once low pressure is reached, reduce the heat to stabilise the pressure and cook for 20 minutes or until the lamb is tender.

• Remove the cooker from the heat and release the pressure using the natural release method. Remove the lid carefully.

• Stir through the lentils and reserved cooking liquid and heat through. Season to taste with salt and freshly ground black pepper and garnish with the rosemary sprigs.

Lamb

# PERSIAN LAMB WITH CHICKPEAS

**preparation time:** 20 minutes
**cooking time:** 55 minutes
**serves:** 4–6

750 g (1 lb 10 oz) boneless lamb leg
   or shoulder
2¹/₂ tablespoons olive oil
200 g (7 oz) eggplant (aubergine),
   cut into 3 cm (1¹/₄ inch) chunks
1 large onion, chopped
2 garlic cloves, chopped
1 teaspoon ground cinnamon
1 teaspoon allspice
1 teaspoon freshly grated nutmeg
250 ml (9 fl oz/1 cup) chicken stock
1 x 400 g (14 oz) tin chopped
   tomatoes

1 tablespoon tomato paste
   (concentrated purée)
60 ml (2 fl oz/¹/₄ cup) lemon juice
1 carrot, chopped
1 zucchini (courgette), chopped
90 g (3¹/₄ oz/³/₄ cup) raisins
1 x 400 g (14 oz) tin chickpeas,
   drained and rinsed (see Note)
60 g (2¹/₄ oz/¹/₂ cup) slivered
   almonds, toasted
1 small handful mint, to garnish

• Trim the lamb of excess fat, cut into 2 cm (³/₄ inch) cubes and season with salt and freshly ground black pepper.

• Heat half the oil in a 6 litre (210 fl oz) pressure cooker over high heat and cook the eggplant for 5 minutes or until well browned and tender. Remove from the cooker and set aside.

• Add the onion to the cooker and cook over medium heat for 5 minutes or until starting to soften. Add the garlic, cinnamon, allspice and nutmeg and cook for a further 2 minutes or until aromatic. Remove from the cooker and set aside.

*Lamb*

● Heat the remaining oil in the cooker over high heat and cook the lamb in batches until well browned on all sides.

● Return all the lamb to the cooker with the onion mixture, stock, tomatoes, tomato paste and lemon juice and stir well. Lock the lid in place and bring the cooker to low pressure over high heat. Once low pressure is reached, reduce the heat to stabilise the pressure and cook for 20 minutes.

● Remove the cooker from the heat and release the pressure using the quick release method. Remove the lid carefully. Stir in the carrot, zucchini and raisins, replace the lid immediately and lock in place. Bring the cooker back to low pressure over high heat. Once low pressure is reached, reduce the heat to stabilise the pressure and cook for 4 minutes or until the lamb and vegetables are tender.

● Remove the cooker from the heat and release the pressure using the natural release method. Remove the lid carefully. Add the chickpeas and eggplant to the cooker and stir through. Cook, uncovered, over medium heat until heated through.

● To serve, spoon into serving bowls and scatter over the almonds and mint. Serve with basmati rice and plain yoghurt if desired.

*Note You can replace the tinned chickpeas with 245 g (9 oz/1 1/2 cups) cooked dried chickpeas (see page 15 for pressure cooking instructions).*

Lamb

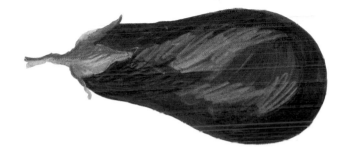

# LAMB KORMA

**preparation time:** 20 minutes
**cooking time:** 50 minutes
**serves:** 6

1 kg (2 lb 4 oz) boneless lamb
   shoulder
2 onions
2 tablespoons desiccated coconut
3 green chillies, roughly chopped
4 garlic cloves, crushed
5 cm (2 inch) piece ginger, grated
50 g (1¾ oz/⅓ cup) cashew nuts
6 cloves
¼ teaspoon ground cinnamon

500 ml (17 fl oz/2 cups) chicken
   stock
2 tablespoons vegetable oil
60 g (2¼ oz/¼ cup) korma paste
6 cardamom pods, crushed
2 tablespoons pouring cream
2 tablespoons Greek-style yoghurt
1 handful coriander (cilantro) leaves,
   to garnish

*Lamb*

• Trim the lamb of excess fat, cut into 2.5 cm (1 inch) cubes and season well with salt
and freshly ground black pepper. Set aside.

• Roughly chop one onion and thinly slice the other. Put the chopped onion, coconut,
chilli, garlic, ginger, cashew nuts, cloves and cinnamon in the bowl of a food processor.
Add a little of the stock and process to a smooth paste.

• Heat half the oil in a 6 litre (210 fl oz) pressure cooker over medium heat and cook
the sliced onion for 5 minutes or until starting to soften. Add the onion and spice
mixture, korma paste and cardamom pods and cook for a further 3 minutes or until
aromatic. Remove from the cooker and set aside.

• Heat the remaining oil in the cooker over high heat and cook the lamb in batches
until well browned on all sides. Remove from the cooker and set aside.

• Return all the lamb to the cooker with the onion mixture and the remaining stock.

Stir well. Lock the lid in place and bring the cooker to high pressure over high heat. Once high pressure is reached, reduce the heat to stabilise the pressure and cook for 20 minutes or until the lamb is tender.

● Remove the cooker from the heat and release the pressure using the natural release method. Remove the lid carefully.

● Stir through the cream and simmer gently until the sauce has reduced slightly. Remove from the heat and stir through the yoghurt. Season to taste with salt and freshly ground black pepper.

● Ladle the curry into serving bowls over steamed rice and sprinkle with the coriander.


# LAMB SHANKS WITH TOMATO, CHILLI AND HONEY

preparation time: 15 minutes
cooking time: 45 minutes
serves: 4

2 tablespoons olive oil
1 large onion, sliced
2 garlic cloves, thinly sliced
2 teaspoons dried oregano
1/2 teaspoon chilli flakes
8 French-trimmed lamb shanks
250 ml (9 fl oz/1 cup) red wine

500 g (1 lb 2 oz/2 cups) tomato
    passata (puréed tomatoes)
90 g (3 1/4 oz/1/4 cup) honey
250 ml (9 fl oz/1 cup) chicken stock
1 tablespoon chopped flat-leaf
    (Italian) parsley

▶

▶ ● Heat half the oil in an 8 litre (280 fl oz) pressure cooker over medium heat and cook the onion for 5 minutes or until starting to soften. Add the garlic, oregano and chilli and cook for a further 2 minutes or until aromatic. Remove from the cooker and set aside.

● Heat the remaining oil in the cooker over high heat and cook the shanks in batches until well browned on all sides. Remove from the cooker and set aside.

● Add the wine to the cooker and simmer for 2 minutes, scraping the base of the pot. Return the shanks to the cooker with the onion mixture, tomato passata, honey and stock and stir well. Lock the lid in place and bring the cooker to high pressure over high heat. Once high pressure is reached, reduce the heat to stabilise the pressure and cook for 25 minutes or until the meat is very tender.

● Remove the cooker from the heat and release the pressure using the natural release method. Remove the lid carefully.

● Stir through the parsley and season with salt and freshly ground black pepper. Serve with steamed rice or couscous.

Lamb

# ROGAN JOSH

preparation time: 20 minutes
cooking time: 55 minutes
serves: 6

1 kg (2 lb 4 oz) boneless lamb
   shoulder
1/2 teaspoon saffron threads
2 tablespoons vegetable oil
1 onion, finely chopped
3 garlic cloves, crushed
6 cm (2 1/2 inch) piece ginger, grated
2 teaspoons ground coriander
2 teaspoons ground cumin
2 teaspoons paprika

1 teaspoon chilli powder
1/2 teaspoon garam masala
6 cardamom pods, crushed
4 cloves
2 bay leaves
1 cinnamon stick
400 ml (14 fl oz) chicken stock
165 g (5 3/4 oz/2/3 cup) plain yoghurt
coriander (cilantro) sprigs, to garnish

- Trim the lamb of excess fat, cut into 4 cm (1 1/2 inch) cubes and season with salt and freshly ground black pepper. Combine the saffron with 1 tablespoon hot water and set aside to soak for 10 minutes.

- Meanwhile, heat half the oil in a 6 litre (210 fl oz) pressure cooker over medium heat and cook the onion for 5 minutes or until starting to soften. Add the garlic, ginger, ground coriander, cumin, paprika, chilli, garam masala, cardamom, cloves, bay leaves and cinnamon stick and cook for a further 2 minutes or until aromatic. Remove from the cooker and set aside.

- Heat the remaining oil in the cooker over high heat and cook the lamb in batches until well browned on all sides. Return all the lamb to the cooker with the saffron mixture, onion mixture and stock and stir well. Lock the lid in place and bring the cooker to low pressure over high heat. Once low pressure is reached, reduce the heat to stabilise the pressure and cook for 25 minutes or until the lamb is tender.

▶

▶ • Remove the cooker from the heat and release the pressure using the natural release method. Remove the lid carefully. Allow to cool slightly.

• Remove all but 150 ml (5 fl oz) of the sauce from the cooker. Add the yoghurt and stir through. Simmer gently for 5 minutes or until thickened slightly. Taste and adjust the seasoning if necessary.

• Serve the curry with steamed rice and garnish with the coriander sprigs.


# TURKISH MEATBALLS

**preparation time:** 20 minutes
**cooking time:** 15 minutes
**serves:** 4

500 g (1 lb 2 oz) minced (ground) lamb
3 teaspoons ground cumin
2 teaspoons ground cinnamon
2 teaspoons ground coriander
1 teaspoon allspice
1 garlic clove, crushed
1 tablespoon olive oil

375 ml (13 fl oz/1$^{1}$/$_{2}$ cups) chicken stock
1 x 400 g (14 oz) tin chopped tomatoes
35 g (1$^{1}$/$_{4}$ oz/$^{1}$/$_{4}$ cup) toasted pistachio nuts
2 tablespoons currants
2 tablespoons chopped coriander (cilantro) leaves

• Put the lamb in a bowl and add 1$^{1}$/$_{2}$ teaspoons of the cumin, 1 teaspoon of the cinnamon, 1 teaspoon of the coriander, all the allspice and the garlic. Season with salt and freshly ground black pepper. Using your hands, mix the spices and lamb together well. Roll the mixture into small balls.

- Heat the oil in a 6 litre (210 fl oz) pressure cooker over medium heat and cook the remaining cumin, cinnamon and coriander for 30 seconds or until aromatic.

- Add the stock and tomatoes to the cooker, season with salt and freshly ground black pepper and stir well. Bring to a simmer over high heat and then add the meatballs. Lock the lid in place and bring the cooker to low pressure over high heat. Once low pressure is reached, reduce the heat to stabilise the pressure and cook for 5 minutes or until the meatballs are cooked through.

- Remove the cooker from the heat and release the pressure using the natural release method. Remove the lid carefully. Taste and adjust the seasoning if necessary. Stir through the pistachios, currants and coriander before serving.

# LAMB SHANKS IN RED WINE

preparation time: 20 minutes
cooking time: 1 hour
serves: 4

Lamb

2 tablespoons olive oil
1 onion, finely diced
1 leek, white part only, finely diced
1 carrot, finely diced
2 celery stalks, finely diced
3 garlic cloves, thinly sliced
4 rosemary sprigs
4 prosciutto slices, chopped

4 lamb shanks (about 300–350 g/ 10 1/2–12 oz each)
250 ml (9 fl oz/1 cup) red wine
500 ml (17 fl oz/2 cups) beef stock
60 g (2 1/4 oz/1/4 cup) tomato paste (concentrated purée)
90 g (3 1/4 oz/1/2 cup) black olives
1 small handful flat-leaf (Italian) parsley leaves, finely chopped

▶

▶ • Heat half the oil in a 6 litre (210 fl oz) pressure cooker over medium heat and cook the onion, leek, carrot and celery for 10 minutes or until starting to soften. Add the garlic and rosemary and cook for a further 2 minutes or until aromatic. Remove from the cooker and set aside.

• Add the prosciutto to the cooker and cook over medium–high heat for 5 minutes or until crisp. Remove from the cooker and set aside.

• Season the shanks with salt and freshly ground black pepper. Heat the remaining oil in the cooker over high heat and cook the shanks until well browned on all sides. Remove from the cooker and set aside.

• Add the wine to the cooker and simmer for 2 minutes, scraping the base of the pot. Stir in the stock and tomato paste. Return the shanks to the cooker with the onion mixture and prosciutto and stir well.

• Lock the lid in place and bring the cooker to high pressure over high heat. Once high pressure is reached, reduce the heat to stabilise the pressure and cook for 30 minutes or until the meat is very tender and almost falling from the bone.

• Remove the cooker from the heat and release the pressure using the natural release method. Remove the lid carefully.

• Add the olives and parsley to the cooker and stir through. Taste and adjust the seasoning if necessary. Serve with boiled potatoes if desired.

*Lamb*

# SPICED LAMB WITH GREEN BEANS

preparation time: 25 minutes
cooking time: 50 minutes
serves: 4

750 g (1 lb 10 oz) boneless lamb
    shoulder
1 tablespoon olive oil
1 large onion, diced
1 carrot, diced
2 celery stalks, leaves reserved, diced
2 garlic cloves, chopped
1 tablespoon grated fresh ginger
1 teaspoon ground coriander
2 teaspoons ground cumin
1/2 teaspoon ground turmeric

pinch chilli flakes
500 ml (17 fl oz/2 cups) chicken stock
250 g (9 oz/1 cup) tomato passata
    (puréed tomatoes) or tomato
    pasta sauce
1 tablespoon lemon juice
200 g (7 oz) green beans, trimmed
    and cut into 4 cm (11/2 inch)
    lengths
1 small handful coriander (cilantro)
    leaves

• Trim the lamb of excess fat, cut into 2 cm (3/4 inch) cubes and season with salt and freshly ground black pepper. Set aside.

• Heat half the oil in a 6 litre (210 fl oz) pressure cooker over medium heat and cook the onion, carrot and celery for 10 minutes or until softened. Add the garlic, ginger, ground coriander, cumin, turmeric and chilli and cook for a further 2 minutes or until aromatic. Remove from the cooker and set aside.

• Heat the remaining oil in the cooker over high heat and cook the lamb in batches until well browned on all sides. Return all the lamb to the cooker with the vegetable mixture, stock, tomato passata and lemon juice and stir well.

• Lock the lid in place and bring the cooker to high pressure over high heat. Once high pressure is reached, reduce the heat to stabilise the pressure and cook for 20 minutes.

▶

*Lamb*

▶ • Remove the cooker from the heat and release the pressure using the natural release method. Remove the lid carefully.

• Add the beans to the cooker and cook, uncovered, over medium heat for 4 minutes or until the beans are tender. Taste and adjust the seasoning if necessary.

• To serve, pile onto plates and garnish with coriander. Serve with basmati rice or warmed flat bread.

# LAMB SHOULDER WITH WHITE BEANS

**preparation time:** 20 minutes
**cooking time:** 50 minutes
**serves:** 4

1 kg (2 lb 4 oz) boned lamb shoulder
2 tablespoons olive oil
2 large onions, chopped
2 carrots, chopped
3 garlic cloves, chopped
185 ml (6 fl oz/3/4 cup) dry red wine
375 ml (13 fl oz/1<sup>1</sup>/2 cups) chicken
   stock

1 bouquet garni (see Notes)
1 x 400 g (14 oz) tin cannellini beans,
   drained and rinsed (see Notes)
1 tablespoon chopped flat-leaf
   (Italian) parsley
lemon wedges, to serve (optional)

• Tie the lamb with kitchen string to keep its shape. Rub the lamb all over with salt and freshly ground black pepper.

• Heat half the oil in an 8 litre (280 fl oz) pressure cooker over medium heat and cook the onion and carrot for 5 minutes or until the onion starts to soften. Add the garlic and cook for a further 2 minutes or until aromatic. Remove from the cooker and set aside.

- Heat the remaining oil in the cooker over high heat and cook the lamb until well browned on all sides. Add the wine and simmer for 2 minutes. Return the onion mixture to the cooker with the stock and bouquet garni and stir well.

- Lock the lid in place and bring the cooker to low pressure over high heat. Once low pressure is reached, reduce the heat to stabilise the pressure and cook for 25 minutes or until the meat is tender.

- Remove the cooker from the heat and release the pressure using the natural release method. Remove the lid carefully.

- Lift the lamb out of the cooker, cover and keep warm. Discard the bouquet garni. Skim the excess fat from the surface of the liquid in the cooker, then add the beans. Cook, uncovered, for 4 minutes, or until the beans are heated through and the sauce has thickened slightly. Season to taste with salt and freshly ground black pepper.

- Carve the lamb in slices and arrange on a platter. Spoon the beans around the lamb and drizzle with the sauce. Sprinkle with parsley and serve with lemon wedges if desired. Serve the remaining sauce separately.

*Notes* *To make a bouquet garni, tie 4 flat-leaf (Italian) parsley sprigs, 4 thyme sprigs and 2 rosemary sprigs together with kitchen string.*
*You can replace the tinned cannellini beans with 240 g (8$\frac{1}{2}$ oz/1$\frac{1}{3}$ cups) cooked dried cannellini beans (see page 15 for pressure cooking instructions).*

Lamb

# Pork

From cassoulet and pork vindaloo
to Asian-style pork belly dishes,
pressure cookers seal in the flavour and
moisture, giving you melt-in-the-mouth
tenderness every time.

# LION'S HEAD MEATBALLS

preparation time: 20 minutes
cooking time: 15 minutes
serves: 4

100 g (3¹/₂ oz) dried rice vermicelli
   noodles
450 g (1 lb) minced (ground) pork
1 egg white
4 spring onions (scallions), finely
   chopped
1 tablespoon Chinese rice wine
1 teaspoon grated fresh ginger

1 tablespoon light soy sauce
2 teaspoons sugar
1 teaspoon sesame oil
white pepper
750 ml (26 fl oz/3 cups) chicken stock
300 g (10¹/₂ oz) bok choy (pak choy),
   sliced

● Put the vermicelli in a heatproof bowl, cover with boiling water and soak for
10 minutes, or until soft. Drain and set aside.

● Meanwhile, put the pork and egg white in a food processor and process briefly
until the mixture is fluffy. Alternatively, mash the pork in a large bowl and gradually
add the egg white, beating well until the mixture is fluffy.

● Add the spring onion, rice wine, ginger, soy sauce, sugar and sesame oil, season
with salt and white pepper, and process or beat again briefly. Roll the mixture into
walnut-sized balls.

● Put the stock into a 6 litre (210 fl oz) pressure cooker and bring to the boil over
high heat. Add the meatballs, lock the lid in place and bring the cooker to low
pressure over high heat. Once low pressure is reached, reduce the heat to stabilise
the pressure and cook for 5 minutes or until the meatballs are cooked.

● Remove the cooker from the heat and release the pressure using the natural
release method. Remove the lid carefully.

▶

Pork

▶ • Add the bok choy and cook, uncovered, over medium heat until the bok choy wilts.

• To serve, divide the noodles among deep serving bowls and ladle the meatballs and some broth over the top.

# PEA AND HAM SOUP

**preparation time:** 25 minutes
**cooking time:** 1 hour 5 minutes
**serves:** 6–8

Pork

1 tablespoon olive oil
2 onions, finely chopped
2 carrots, finely chopped
2 celery stalks, finely chopped
1 turnip, finely chopped
3 garlic cloves, crushed
2 bay leaves

2 thyme sprigs
1 smoked ham hock (about 800 g/
   1 lb 12 oz)
1 litre (35 fl oz/4 cups) chicken stock
440 g (15$^1$/$_2$ oz/2 cups) split green
   peas, rinsed and drained

• Heat the oil in an 8 litre (280 fl oz) pressure cooker over medium heat and cook the onion, carrot, celery and turnip for 10 minutes or until the onion is soft. Add the garlic, bay leaves and thyme and cook for a further 2 minutes or until aromatic.

• Add the ham hock, stock and 1.25 litres (44 fl oz/5 cups) water and stir well. Lock the lid in place and bring the cooker to high pressure over high heat. Once high pressure is reached, reduce the heat to stabilise the pressure and cook for 40 minutes.

• Remove the cooker from the heat and release the pressure using the quick release method. Remove the lid carefully.

• Stir in the split peas, replace the lid immediately and lock in place. Bring the cooker back to high pressure over high heat. Once high pressure is reached, reduce the heat to stabilise the pressure and cook for a further 10 minutes or until the ham is falling off the bone and the peas are very soft.

• Remove the cooker from the heat and release the pressure using the natural release method. Remove the lid carefully. Allow the soup to cool slightly.

• Remove the ham bone and meat from the cooker. When cool enough to handle, discard the skin and remove any meat still attached to the bone, then shred the meat into small pieces. Return the meat to the soup. Season to taste with freshly ground black pepper and serve.

*note* *If the soup is a little thick, stir through 125 ml–250 ml (4 fl oz–9 fl oz/ $1/2$ –1 cup) extra chicken stock.*

# CABBAGE ROLLS

preparation time: 25 minutes
cooking time: 20 minutes
serves: 4

1 large cabbage
1 tablespoon vegetable oil
2 bacon slices, finely diced
400 g (14 oz) minced (ground) pork
75 g ($2^3/4$ oz/$3/4$ cup) dry breadcrumbs
3 garlic cloves, crushed
1 egg, lightly beaten
1 onion, finely diced

2 tablespoons chopped flat-leaf (Italian) parsley
1 tablespoon dijon mustard
1 tablespoon Worcestershire sauce
2 tablespoons red wine vinegar
$1/4$ teaspoon ground white pepper
500 g (1 lb 2 oz/2 cups) tomato passata (puréed tomatoes)
125 ml (4 fl oz/$1/2$ cup) chicken stock

▶

▶ ● Cut the cabbage in half and place in a large heatproof bowl. Pour over boiling water to cover. Set aside for 5–10 minutes or until you can separate the cabbage leaves with kitchen tongs. Refresh the leaves in cold water and drain.

● To make the filling, heat half the oil in a 6 litre (210 fl oz) pressure cooker over medium–high heat and cook half the bacon for 5 minutes or until crisp. Transfer the bacon to a large bowl. Add the pork, breadcrumbs, two-thirds of the garlic, the egg, onion, 1 tablespoon of the parsley, the mustard, Worcestershire sauce, half the vinegar, the white pepper and 1 1/2 teaspoons salt to the bowl. Mix well.

● Use the larger cabbage leaves to roll the parcels, and set the smaller leaves aside for later. Cut a 'V' shape to remove the large connecting vein in each cabbage leaf. Form some of the pork stuffing mixture into a sausage shape, about 2 cm ( 3/4 inch) thick and 4 cm (1 1/2 inches) long, and place it in the middle of a cabbage leaf. Roll the cabbage up around the pork, making sure the filling is completely covered. Continue until all the large leaves are used.

● Shred four of the reserved smaller leaves and set aside. Heat the remaining oil in the cooker over medium–high heat and cook the remaining bacon for 3 minutes or until starting to brown. Add the remaining garlic and cook for 1 minute or until aromatic. Add the shredded cabbage, tomato passata, stock and remaining vinegar. Season with salt and freshly ground black pepper. Bring to a simmer over high heat. Stir well.

● Place the cabbage rolls into the pressure cooker's steaming basket or on a trivet and place into the cooker. Lock the lid in place and bring the cooker to low pressure over high heat. Once low pressure is reached, reduce the heat to stabilise the pressure and cook for 7 minutes or until the pork filling is cooked through.

● Remove the cooker from the heat and release the pressure using the natural release method. Remove the lid carefully.

● Serve the rolls with the sauce and sprinkled with the remaining parsley.

Pork

# BOSTON-STYLE BAKED BEANS WITH HAM

**preparation time:** 20 minutes
**cooking time:** 1 hour 10 minutes
**serves:** 6

1 tablespoon olive oil
1 large onion, finely chopped
1 garlic clove
1 bay leaf
1.5 kg (3 lb 5 oz) ham hock
60 ml (2 fl oz/¼ cup) molasses
80 g (2¾ oz/⅓ cup firmly packed)
   soft brown sugar

160 g (5½ oz/⅔ cup) tomato paste
   (concentrated purée)
2 tablespoons Worcestershire sauce
1 teaspoon mustard powder
2 x 400 g (14 oz) tins cannellini
   beans, drained and rinsed
   (see Note)

● Heat the oil in a 6 litre (210 fl oz) pressure cooker over medium heat and cook the onion for 10 minutes or until softened. Add the garlic and bay leaf and cook for a further 2 minutes or until aromatic.

● Add the ham hock, molasses, brown sugar, tomato paste, Worcestershire sauce, mustard and 1.25 litres (44 fl oz/5 cups) water to the cooker and stir well. Lock the lid in place and bring the cooker to high pressure over high heat. Once high pressure is reached, reduce the heat to stabilise the pressure and cook for 50 minutes or until the ham is falling off the bone.

● Remove the cooker from the heat and release the pressure using the natural release method. Remove the lid carefully. Allow to cool slightly.

● Remove the ham bone and meat from the pressure cooker. When cool enough to handle, discard the skin and remove any meat still attached to the bone, then shred the meat into small pieces. Return the meat to the slow cooker with the cannellini beans and stir to combine well.

Pork

▶

▶ • Simmer, uncovered, until the sauce is thick and syrupy. Taste and season with salt and freshly ground black pepper if necessary. Serve with thick buttered toast or cornbread to mop up the juices.

*Note* *You can replace the tinned cannellini beans with 480 g (1 lb1 oz/2²/3 cups) cooked dried cannellini beans (see page 15 for pressure cooking intrustions).*

# SPARE RIBS WITH BEER AND BARBECUE SAUCE

**preparation time:** 20 minutes
**cooking time:** 30 minutes
**serves:** 4–6

1.5 kg (3 lb 5 oz) pork spare ribs
185 ml (6 fl oz/³/4 cup) beer
185 ml (6 fl oz/³/4 cup) barbecue sauce
1 tablespoon Worcestershire sauce
2 tablespoons sweet chilli sauce
¹/2 teaspoon sweet paprika
pinch cayenne pepper

2 garlic cloves, crushed
4 thyme sprigs
1 bay leaf
300 ml (10¹/2 fl oz) chicken stock
1 tablespoon cornflour (cornstarch)
1 small handful coriander (cilantro)
    leaves, to garnish

• Cut the ribs into individual ribs, or into sets of two or three if preferred, and trim away any excess fat.

• In a large bowl, combine the beer, barbecue sauce, Worcestershire sauce, sweet chilli sauce, paprika, cayenne and garlic. Season with salt and freshly ground black pepper. Add the ribs and stir to coat in the sauce (see Note).

• Transfer the ribs and marinade, thyme, bay leaf and stock to an 8 litre (280 fl oz)

Pork

pressure cooker. Bring to the boil over high heat. Lock the lid in place and bring the cooker to high pressure over high heat. Once high pressure is reached, reduce the heat to stabilise the pressure and cook for 20 minutes or until the meat is tender.

● Remove the cooker from the heat and release the pressure using the natural release method. Remove the lid carefully. Using kitchen tongs, remove the ribs to a plate and cover to keep warm. Skim off any fat from the surface of the sauce. Mix the cornflour with 1 tablespoon water and stir into the sauce. Cook over medium heat, uncovered, until the sauce has thickened.

● Serve the ribs piled onto plates and spoon over some of the sauce. Sprinkle over the coriander leaves. Supply lots of paper napkins for sticky fingers.

Note *If time permits, marinate the ribs overnight in the fridge.*

# SPANISH-STYLE PORK AND VEGETABLE STEW

**preparation time:** 20 minutes
**cooking time:** 1 hour
**serves:** 4–6

1 kg (2 lb 4 oz) boneless pork
   shoulder
2 teaspoons olive oil
2 hot chorizo sausages, sliced
1 red onion, diced
2 red capsicums (peppers), seeded
   and chopped
2 garlic cloves, chopped
125 ml (4 fl oz/$^{1}/_{2}$ cup) white wine
200 ml (7 fl oz) chicken stock
2 tablespoons sherry

600 g (1 lb 5 oz) all-purpose
   potatoes, peeled and cubed
1 x 400 g (14 oz) tin chopped tomatoes
60 g ($2^{1}/_{4}$ oz/$^{1}/_{4}$ cup) tomato paste
   (concentrated purée)
pinch saffron threads
1 tablespoon sweet paprika
10 large thyme sprigs
1 bay leaf
1 handful flat-leaf (Italian) parsley,
   chopped

Pork

▶ • Trim the pork and cut it into 4 cm (1 1/2 inch) cubes. Heat the oil in an 8 litre (280 fl oz) pressure cooker over medium–high heat and cook the chorizo for 5 minutes or until golden. Remove with a slotted spoon. Add a third of the pork to the cooker and cook for 5 minutes or until browned. Remove from the cooker and repeat with the remaining pork in two more batches. Set the chorizo and pork aside.

• Remove almost all of the oil from the cooker. Add the onion and capsicum to the cooker and cook over medium heat for 5 minutes. Add the garlic and cook until aromatic. Add the wine and simmer for 1–2 minutes, scraping the base of the pot.

• Return the pork and chorizo to the cooker with the stock, sherry, potato, tomatoes, tomato paste, saffron, paprika, thyme and bay leaf. Bring to the boil over high heat. Lock the lid in place and bring the cooker to high pressure over high heat. Once high pressure is reached, reduce the heat to stabilise the pressure and cook for 25 minutes or until the pork is tender.

• Remove the cooker from the heat and release the pressure using the natural release method. Season to taste with salt and freshly ground black pepper. Stir through the parsley and serve.

# PORK NECK WITH ORANGE AND STAR ANISE

**preparation time:** 25 minutes
**cooking time:** 40 minutes
**serves:** 6–8

1 large handful flat-leaf (Italian)
  parsley
2 teaspoons ground cinnamon
1 tablespoon grated fresh ginger
2 garlic cloves, crushed
1 orange

1.6 kg (3 lb 8 oz) rolled pork neck
  (pork scotch) fillet
2 tablespoons olive oil
250 ml (9 fl oz/1 cup) chicken stock
1 star anise

• Put the parsley in a heatproof bowl and pour over enough boiling water to cover. Strain, reserving some of the water, then transfer the blanched parsley to the small bowl of a food processor along with the cinnamon, ginger and garlic. Process to a paste, adding a little of the reserved water if necessary. Season with salt and freshly ground black pepper.

• Peel and segment the orange. Cut the pork lengthways along the middle and open it out flat on a clean work surface. Brush with the parsley and cinnamon paste and lay the orange segments along the centre. Roll the pork tightly to form a cylinder, enclosing the orange, and tie at intervals with kitchen string. Brush the pork with half the oil and generously season with salt and freshly ground black pepper.

• Heat the remaining oil in an 8 litre (280 fl oz) pressure cooker over high heat and seal the pork until golden all over (see Note).

• Add the stock and star anise to the cooker. Bring the stock to the boil over high heat. Lock the lid in place and bring the cooker to low pressure over high heat. Once low pressure is reached, reduce the heat to stabilise the pressure and cook for 25 minutes or until the pork is tender.

• Season with salt and freshly ground black pepper. Serve the pork with mashed sweet potato.

*Note If the base of your pressure cooker is too small to accommodate the pork, you can seal it in a large frying pan and then transfer it to the pressure cooker with the stock and star anise.*

Pork

# SPICY SAUSAGE AND BEAN CASSEROLE

**preparation time:** 20 minutes
**cooking time:** 30 minutes
**serves:** 6

6 thick pork sausages
6 bacon slices, cut into 6 cm
   (2¹/₂ inch) strips
1 tablespoon olive oil
4 small onions, quartered
10 garlic cloves, peeled
3 bay leaves
7 oregano sprigs, leaves only
1 small red chilli, split and seeded

3 long thin carrots, cut into 3 cm
   (1¹/₄ inch) pieces
500 ml (17 fl oz/2 cups) chicken stock
2 tablespoons tomato paste
   (concentrated purée)
2 x 400 g (1 lb 12 oz) tins red kidney
   beans, drained and rinsed
   (see Note)
1 x 400 g (14 oz) tins cannellini beans,
   drained and rinsed (see Note)

• Prick the sausages all over. Cook the sausages, uncovered, in a 6 litre (210 fl oz) pressure cooker over medium–high heat until browned all over. Remove the sausages from the cooker and set aside.

• Add the bacon to the cooker and cook over medium–high heat for 5 minutes or until crisp. Remove from the cooker and set aside.

• Add the oil and onion to the cooker and cook over medium heat for 5 minutes or until starting to soften. Add the garlic, bay leaves, half the oregano and the chilli and cook for a further 2 minutes or until aromatic.

• Return the sausages and bacon to the cooker with the carrot, stock and tomato paste and stir well. Season well with freshly ground black pepper. Lock the lid in place and bring the cooker to high pressure over high heat. Once high pressure is reached, reduce the heat to stabilise the pressure and cook for 7 minutes or until the sausages are cooked through.

- Remove the cooker from the heat and release the pressure using the natural release method. Remove the lid carefully.

- Stir in the kidney beans and cannellini beans and simmer, uncovered and stirring occasionally, until the sauce has thickened slightly. Stir and taste for seasoning. Sprinkle the remaining oregano over the casserole just before serving.

*Note* *You can replace the tinned beans with 500 g (1 lb 2 oz/2²/3 cups) cooked dried kidney beans and 240 g (8¹/2 oz/1¹/3 cups) cooked dried cannellini beans (see page 15 for cooking instructions).*

# PORK CUTLETS WITH PANCETTA AND SWEET POTATO

**preparation time:** 15 minutes
**cooking time:** 25 minutes
**serves:** 4

4 pork cutlets
1 tablespoon olive oil
90 g (3¹/4 oz) piece pancetta,
   1 cm (¹/2 inch) thick, diced
6 bulb spring onions (scallions),
   trimmed with 3 cm (1¹/4 inch)
   stems, halved lengthways
2 garlic cloves, chopped
1 cinnamon stick

350 g (12 oz) purple-skinned sweet
   potato, peeled, cut into 5 cm
   (2 inch) chunks
250 ml (9 fl oz/1 cup) chicken stock
250 ml (9 fl oz/1 cup) sparkling apple
   juice (cider)
2 tablespoons chopped flat-leaf
   (Italian) parsley

- Trim the pork of any excess fat. Season with salt and freshly ground black pepper. Heat the oil in an 8 litre (280 fl oz) pressure cooker over medium–high heat and cook the cutlets until well browned on both sides. Remove and set aside.

▶

▶ ● Add the diced pancetta and spring onions to the cooker and cook over medium–high heat until the spring onions start to colour. Add the garlic and cinnamon stick and cook for 1 minute or until aromatic.

● Return the pork to the cooker with the sweet potato, stock and sparkling apple juice. Lock the lid in place and bring the cooker to low pressure over high heat. Once low pressure is reached, reduce the heat to stabilise the pressure and cook for 8 minutes or until the pork is tender.

● Remove the cooker from the heat and release the pressure using the natural release method.

● Transfer the pork and vegetables to a serving platter. Cover with foil and set aside. Remove the cinnamon stick. Simmer the sauce, uncovered, until thickened slightly. Serve the pork with the vegetables and the sauce. Scatter over the parsley.

*Pork*

# PORK LOIN WITH CABBAGE AND POTATO

**preparation time:** 20 minutes
**cooking time:** 55 minutes
**serves:** 6

2 teaspoons fennel seeds
2 teaspoons caraway seeds
1 teaspoon sea salt
1/2 teaspoon sweet paprika
1.2 kg (2 lb 10 oz) boned, rolled
   pork loin
1 tablespoon olive oil
1 bacon slice, cut into small dice
1 small onion, thinly sliced

1 tablespoon dijon mustard
125 ml (4 fl oz/1/2 cup) dry white wine
560 ml (191/4 fl oz/21/4 cups) chicken
   stock
1 tablespoon vinegar
700 g (1 lb 9 oz) all-purpose potatoes,
   cut into 3 cm (11/4 inch) chunks
1/2 small red cabbage, finely shredded
125 ml (4 fl oz/1/2 cup) pouring cream

- Using a mortar and pestle or spice grinder, crush or grind the fennel seeds, caraway seeds, sea salt and paprika. Push three-quarters of the spice mixture inside the rolled pork, through the gaps at either end. Sprinkle the remaining spice mixture over the pork.

- Heat the oil in an 8 litre (280 fl oz) pressure cooker over medium heat and cook the pork until well browned on all sides. Remove from the cooker and set aside.

- Add the bacon and onion to the cooker and cook over medium heat for 5 minutes or until the onion starts to soften. Add the mustard, wine, stock and vinegar and stir to combine.

- Return the pork to the cooker. Lock the lid in place and bring the cooker to low pressure over high heat. Once low pressure is reached, reduce the heat to stabilise the pressure and cook for 25 minutes.

- Remove the cooker from the heat and release the pressure using the quick release method. Remove the lid carefully.

- Add the potato and cabbage to the cooker, replace the lid immediately and lock in place. Bring the cooker back to low pressure over high heat. Once low pressure is reached, reduce the heat to stabilise the pressure and cook for a further 10 minutes or until the pork is tender and the potatoes are cooked. Remove the cooker from the heat and release the pressure using the natural release method. Transfer the pork to a board and set aside in a warm place.

- Meanwhile, add the cream to the sauce in the cooker and warm through over medium heat. Serve the pork in slices with the potato and cabbage and sauce.

Pork

# PORK WITH ONION AND BARBECUE SAUCE

**preparation time:** 20 minutes (+ 2 hours marinating)
**cooking time:** 40 minutes
**serves:** 4–6

1.5 kg (3 lb 5 oz) pork neck (pork
   scotch) fillet
250 g (9 oz/1 cup) barbecue sauce
1¹/₂ tablespoons roughly chopped
   jalapeño chilli
¹/₂ teaspoon ground cumin
¹/₄ teaspoon ground cinnamon
1 teaspoon sweet paprika
45 g (1¹/₂ oz/¹/₄ cup) soft brown sugar

2 garlic cloves, chopped
1 teaspoon dijon mustard
2 tablespoons red wine vinegar
2 teaspoons Worcestershire sauce
1 tablespoon olive oil
1 onion, thinly sliced
350 ml (12 fl oz) chicken stock
1 tablespoon coriander (cilantro)
   leaves, chopped

- Trim the pork and cut into 3 cm (1¹/₄ inch) cubes.

- Put the barbecue sauce, jalapeño, cumin, cinnamon, paprika, brown sugar, garlic, mustard, vinegar and Worcestershire sauce in a large bowl. Add 250 ml (9 fl oz/1 cup) water and stir to combine. Add the pork and stir to coat in the marinade. Cover and refrigerate for 2 hours.

- Heat the oil in a 6 litre (210 fl oz) pressure cooker over medium heat and cook the onion for 5 minutes or until starting to soften.

- Add the pork with the marinade and the stock to the cooker and stir well. Lock the lid in place and bring the cooker to high pressure over high heat. Once high pressure is reached, reduce the heat to stabilise the pressure and cook for 35 minutes or until the pork is tender.

- Remove the cooker from the heat and release the pressure using the natural release method. Remove the lid carefully. Serve sprinkled with the coriander.

Pork

# JAPANESE PORK BELLY

**preparation time:** 15 minutes
**cooking time:** 40 minutes
**serves:** 4–6

1 kg (2 lb 4 oz) boneless, skinless
    pork belly
1 tablespoon olive oil
100 g (3$^1$/$_2$ oz) ginger, cut into long
    matchsticks
500 ml (17 fl oz/2 cups) dashi
    (made up according to packet
    instructions)

170 ml (5$^1$/$_2$ fl oz/$^2$/$_3$ cup) sake
60 ml (2 fl oz/$^1$/$_4$ cup) mirin
2 tablespoons dark brown sugar
125 ml (4 fl oz/$^1$/$_2$ cup) Japanese
    soy sauce
Japanese mustard, to serve (optional)
*wasabi*

- Trim the pork of excess fat, cut into 5 cm (2 inch) cubes and season with salt and freshly ground black pepper. Heat the oil in a 6 litre (210 fl oz) pressure cooker over high heat and cook the pork in batches until well browned.

- Return all the pork to the cooker with the ginger, dashi, sake, mirin, brown sugar and soy sauce. Pour in 375 ml (13 fl oz/1 1/2 cups) water and stir well. Lock the lid in place and bring the cooker to high pressure over high heat. Once high pressure is reached, reduce the heat to stabilise the pressure and cook for 25 minutes or until the pork is very tender.

- Remove the cooker from the heat and release the pressure using the natural release method. Remove the lid carefully.

- Serve with Japanese mustard on the side if desired and steamed rice.

Pork

# PORK VINDALOO

**preparation time:** 25 minutes (+ 3 hours marinating)
**cooking time:** 40 minutes
**serves:** 4

6 cardamom pods
1 teaspoon black peppercorns
4 dried chillies
1 teaspoon cloves
10 cm (4 inch) piece cinnamon stick, roughly broken
1 teaspoon cumin seeds
$1/2$ teaspoon coriander seeds
$1/4$ teaspoon fenugreek seeds
$1/2$ teaspoon ground turmeric
80 ml ($2^{1}/2$ fl oz/$^{1}/3$ cup) white wine vinegar
1 tablespoon balsamic vinegar

800 g (1 lb 12 oz) boneless pork shoulder
1 tablespoon peanut oil
2 onions, thinly sliced
10 garlic cloves, thinly sliced
5 cm (2 inch) piece ginger, cut into matchsticks
375 ml (13 fl oz/$1^{1}/2$ cups) chicken stock
250 g (9 oz/1 cup) tomato passata (puréed tomatoes)
4 green chillies, seeded and chopped
1 teaspoon grated palm sugar (jaggery) or soft brown sugar

• Split open the cardamom pods and remove the seeds. Using a mortar and pestle or a spice grinder, finely pound or grind the cardamom seeds, peppercorns, dried chillies, cloves, cinnamon stick, cumin seeds, coriander seeds, fenugreek seeds and turmeric. In a large bowl, mix the ground spices together with the wine vinegar and balsamic vinegar.

• Trim the pork of excess fat, then cut into 2.5 cm (1 inch) cubes. Add the pork to the spice mixture and mix thoroughly to coat well. Cover and marinate in the refrigerator for 3 hours.

*Pork*

- Heat the oil in a 6 litre (210 fl oz) pressure cooker over medium heat and cook the onion for 10 minutes or until softened. Add the garlic and ginger and cook for a further 2 minutes or until aromatic.

- Add the pork to the cooker with the stock, tomato passata, chilli and sugar and stir well. Lock the lid in place and bring the cooker to high pressure over high heat. Once high pressure is reached, reduce the heat to stabilise the pressure and cook for 25 minutes or until the pork is very tender.

- Remove the cooker from the heat and release the pressure using the natural release method. Remove the lid carefully. Serve with steamed rice.

# ADOBE PORK

**preparation time:** 15 minutes
**cooking time:** 55 minutes
**serves:** 6

1 kg (2 lb 4 oz) pork neck (pork
   scotch) fillet
2 tablespoons peanut oil
1 red onion, sliced
2 garlic cloves, chopped
1 tablespoon shredded fresh ginger

2 bay leaves
250 ml (9 fl oz/1 cup) beef stock
125 ml (4 fl oz/1/2 cup) light soy sauce
1 1/2 tablespoons apple cider vinegar
2 tablespoons soft brown sugar
1 1/2 tablespoons lime juice

- Cut the pork into 4 cm (1 1/2 inch) pieces and season with salt and freshly ground black pepper.

- Heat half the oil in a 6 litre (210 fl oz) pressure cooker over medium heat and cook the onion for 5 minutes or until starting to soften. Add the garlic and ginger and cook for a further 2 minutes or until aromatic. Remove from the cooker and set aside.

▶ ● Heat the remaining oil in the cooker over high heat and cook the pork in batches until well browned on all sides.

● Return all the pork to the cooker with the onion mixture, bay leaves, stock, soy sauce, vinegar and brown sugar and stir well. Lock the lid in place and bring the cooker to high pressure over high heat. Once high pressure is reached, reduce the heat to stabilise the pressure and cook for 35 minutes or until the pork is tender.

● Remove the cooker from the heat and release the pressure using the natural release method. Remove the lid carefully. Stir through the lime juice and season to taste with salt and freshly ground black pepper. Serve with steamed rice.

# CASSOULET

**preparation time:** 25 minutes
**cooking time:** 50 minutes
**serves:** 4

4 pork spare ribs (about 600 g/
   1 lb 5 oz)
4 thick (450 g/1 lb) beef or lamb
   sausages
2 tablespoons olive oil
6 French shallots, peeled and
   chopped
1 carrot, diced
1 celery stalk, diced
4 garlic cloves, chopped
1 teaspoon sweet paprika
1 large rosemary sprig or
   1/2 teaspoon dried rosemary

60 ml (2 fl oz/1/4 cup) dry white wine
60 ml (2 fl oz/1/4 cup) chicken stock
1 x 400 g (14 oz) tin chopped
   tomatoes
2 tablespoons tomato paste
   (concentrated purée)
2 x 400 g (14 oz) tins white beans,
   such as cannellini, haricot
   or butter beans, drained and
   rinsed (see Note)
1 small handful flat-leaf (Italian)
   parsley or celery leaves, chopped

*Pork*

● Prepare the spare ribs by removing the rind and excess fat. Cut each spare rib into three thick chunks. Cut the sausages in half.

● Heat half the oil in a 6 litre (210 fl oz) pressure cooker over medium heat and cook the French shallots, carrot and celery for 10 minutes or until starting to soften. Add the garlic, paprika and rosemary and cook for a further 2 minutes or until aromatic. Remove from the cooker and set aside.

● Heat the remaining oil in the cooker over high heat and cook the ribs in batches until well browned on all sides. Remove from the cooker and set aside.

● Add the sausages to the cooker and cook over medium–high heat until browned all over. Remove from the cooker and set aside.

● Add the wine to the cooker and simmer for 2 minutes, scraping the base of the pot. Return the ribs, sausages and French shallot mixture to the cooker with the stock, tomatoes and tomato paste. Season with freshly ground black pepper and stir well.

● Lock the lid in place and bring the cooker to high pressure over high heat. Once high pressure is reached, reduce the heat to stabilise the pressure and cook for 20 minutes or until the ribs are tender. Remove the cooker from the heat and release the pressure using the natural release method. Remove the lid carefully. Stir in the beans and simmer, uncovered, until heated through.

● Taste and season with salt and freshly ground black pepper. Remove the rosemary sprig and stir through the parsley or celery leaves. Serve with crusty bread.

*Note* *You can replace the tinned beans with 480 g (1 lb1 oz/2²/3 cups) cooked dried cannellini beans (see page 15 for cooking instructions).*

Pork

# PORK AND MUSHROOM HOTPOT

**preparation time:** 15 minutes
**cooking time:** 15 minutes
**serves:** 4

500 g (1 lb 2 oz) pork fillet

15 g (1/2 oz) dried Chinese
mushrooms, sliced

1 1/2 tablespoons hoisin sauce

2 teaspoons grated fresh ginger

3 garlic cloves, crushed

1 cinnamon stick

2 star anise

2 tablespoons dark soy sauce

1 tablespoon light soy sauce

2 tablespoons Chinese rice wine

250 ml (9 fl oz/1 cup) chicken stock

1 x 140 g (5 oz) tin straw mushrooms,
rinsed and drained

1 x 125 g (4 1/2 oz) tin sliced bamboo
shoots, drained

shredded spring onions (scallions),
to garnish

• Cut the pork into very thin slices (see Note). Cover and refrigerate.

• Put the dried mushrooms, hoisin sauce, ginger, garlic, cinnamon stick, star anise, dark and light soy sauces, rice wine, stock and 250 ml (9 fl oz/1 cup) water in a 6 litre (210 fl oz) pressure cooker. Lock the lid in place and bring the cooker to high pressure over high heat. Once high pressure is reached, reduce the heat to stabilise the pressure and cook for 10 minutes.

• Remove the cooker from the heat and release the pressure using the quick release method. Remove the lid carefully.

• Stir in the sliced pork, straw mushrooms and bamboo shoots. Cook over medium heat, uncovered, until the pork is just cooked. Garnish with the spring onion and serve with steamed rice and Asian greens.

*Note* *To make it easier to slice the pork very thinly, wrap it in plastic wrap and freeze for 1–2 hours, or until firm, before slicing.*

# RED-COOKED PORK BELLY

**preparation time:** 15 minutes
**cooking time:** 50 minutes
**serves:** 4

500 ml (17 fl oz/2 cups) chicken stock
60 ml (2 fl oz/¼ cup) dark soy sauce
60 ml (2 fl oz/¼ cup) Chinese rice wine
6 dried shiitake mushrooms
4 garlic cloves, bruised
5 cm x 5 cm (2 inch x 2 inch) piece ginger, sliced
1 piece dried mandarin or tangerine peel

2 teaspoons Sichuan peppercorns
2 star anise
1 cinnamon stick
2 tablespoons Chinese rock sugar (see Note)
1 teaspoon sesame oil
1 kg (2 lb 4 oz) pork belly
3 spring onions (scallions), thinly sliced diagonally

- Put 250 ml (9 fl oz/1 cup) water, the stock, soy sauce, rice wine, mushrooms, garlic, ginger, mandarin peel, peppercorns, star anise, cinnamon stick, rock sugar and sesame oil in an 8 litre (280 fl oz) pressure cooker and stir well until the sugar dissolves.

- Add the pork to the cooker. Lock the lid in place and bring the cooker to high pressure over high heat. Once high pressure is reached, reduce the heat to stabilise the pressure and cook for 40 minutes or until the pork is very tender.

- Remove the cooker from the heat and release the pressure using the natural release method. Remove the lid carefully.

- Remove the pork from the liquid in the cooker, cover and set aside. Strain the liquid into a bowl, set the mushrooms aside, then return the strained liquid to the pressure cooker. Simmer, uncovered, until the sauce has thickened slightly. Return the mushrooms to the sauce to heat through.

▶

▶ • Cut the pork into 1 cm (¹/₂ inch) thick slices. Transfer the pork to a platter and spoon over the mushrooms and some of the sauce. Garnish with the spring onion and serve with steamed rice.

*Note* *Chinese rock sugar is a crystallised form of pure sugar and is named for its irregular rock-shaped pieces. It imparts a rich flavour, especially to braised or 'red-cooked' foods, and gives them a translucent glaze. Rock sugar is sold in Asian grocery stores.*

Pork

# Seafood

Super fast and flavoursome is what you get when cooking seafood in a pressure cooker.

# SEAFOOD CHOWDER

**preparation time:** 15 minutes
**cooking time:** 35 minutes
**serves:** 4–6

500 g (1 lb 2 oz) skinless firm white
    fish fillets (see Note)
1 tablespoon olive oil
2 leeks, white part only, thinly sliced
3 large garlic cloves, crushed
1 bay leaf
3 thyme sprigs
100 g (3½ oz) smoked ham,
    diced
1 litre (35 fl oz/4 cups) fish stock

850 g (1 lb 14 oz) all-purpose
    potatoes, peeled and cut into
    2 cm (¾ inch) dice
20 scallops (about 350 g/12 oz),
    without roe
1 x 290 g (10¼ oz) tin baby clams,
    undrained
250 ml (9 fl oz/1 cup) thickened
    cream
2 tablespoons chopped flat-leaf
    (Italian) parsley

● Cut the fish into 4 cm (1½ inch) chunks, then cover and refrigerate until needed.

● Heat the oil in a 6 litre (210 fl oz) pressure cooker over medium heat and cook the leek for 10 minutes or until softened. Add the garlic, bay leaf and thyme and cook for a further 2 minutes or until aromatic. Remove from the cooker and set aside.

● Add the ham to the cooker, increase the heat to medium–high and cook until crisp. Return the leek mixture to the cooker with the stock and potato and stir well. Lock the lid in place and bring the cooker to low pressure over high heat. Once low pressure is reached, reduce the heat to stabilise the pressure and cook for 12 minutes or until the potatoes are very soft.

● Remove the cooker from the heat and release the pressure using the quick release method. Remove the lid carefully and cool slightly.

*Seafood*

- Mash the potatoes until smooth. Stir in the fish, scallops, clams with their liquid and the cream. Simmer for 2–4 minutes or until the fish and scallops are just cooked through.

- Season to taste with salt and freshly ground black pepper. Stir in the parsley and serve with bread.

*Note* *You can use any firm white fish fillets, such as swordfish or gemfish.*

# TOM YUM

**preparation time:** 15 minutes
**cooking time:** 20 minutes
**serves:** 4

3 lemon grass stems, white part only
5–7 bird's eye chillies
1 tablespoon peanut oil
3 thin slices galangal
2 litres (70 fl oz/8 cups) chicken stock
   or water
3 kaffir lime leaves, torn
350 g (12 oz) raw prawns (shrimp)

90 g (3¼ oz/½ cup) drained tinned
   straw mushrooms, or quartered
   button mushrooms
2 tablespoons fish sauce
60 ml (2 fl oz/¼ cup) lime juice
2 teaspoons caster (superfine) sugar
coriander (cilantro) leaves, to garnish

- Use the handle of a knife or a rolling pin to bruise the lemon grass stems. Remove the stems from the chillies and bruise them with the knife handle or rolling pin.

- Heat the oil in a 6 litre (210 fl oz) pressure cooker over medium heat and cook the lemon grass, chillies and galangal for 3 minutes or until aromatic. Add the stock and lime leaves and bring to the boil over high heat. Lock the lid in place and bring the cooker to high pressure over high heat. Once high pressure is reached, reduce ▶

▶ the heat to stabilise the pressure and cook for 10 minutes. Remove the cooker from the heat and release the pressure using the quick release method. Remove the lid carefully.

- Meanwhile, prepare the prawns. Peel the prawns, leaving the tails intact. Gently pull out the dark vein from each prawn back, starting at the head end.

- Add the prawns and mushrooms to the cooker, replace the lid immediately and lock in place. Bring the cooker to low pressure over high heat. Once low pressure is reached, reduce the heat to stabilise the pressure and cook for a further 1 minute, or until the prawns are just cooked.

- Remove the cooker from the heat again and release the pressure using the quick release method. Remove the lid carefully.

- Stir through the fish sauce, lime juice and sugar. Taste, then adjust the seasoning with extra lime juice or fish sauce if necessary. Garnish the soup with the coriander before serving.

# ZARZUELA

preparation time: 35 minutes
cooking time: 35 minutes
serves: 6

500 g (1 lb 2 oz) skinless firm white
    fish fillets, such as swordfish,
    monkfish or gemfish
500 g (1 lb 2 oz) small squid tubes
12 mussels
12 clams (vongole)
12 raw prawns (shrimp)
1 tablespoon olive oil
1 leek, white part only, thinly sliced
1 red capsicum (pepper), seeded and
    thinly sliced
1 green capsicum (pepper), seeded
    and thinly sliced
3 garlic cloves, thinly sliced
1 small red chilli, seeded and
    chopped
2 teaspoons paprika
1 bay leaf
250 ml (9 fl oz/1 cup) dry white wine
large pinch saffron threads
1.5 litres (52 fl oz/6 cups) fish
    or chicken stock

60 ml (2 fl oz/$^1/_4$ cup) brandy
    or Cognac
2 tablespoons lemon juice
1 x 400 g (14 oz) tin chopped
    tomatoes
3 large flat leaf (Italian) parsley sprigs
1 tablespoon chopped flat-leaf
    (Italian) parsley
lemon wedges, to serve

## ROMESCO SAUCE
80 g (2$^3/_4$ oz/$^1/_2$ cup) blanched
    almonds
285 g (10 oz) jar roasted red
    capsicums (peppers), drained
    and rinsed
2 teaspoons sweet paprika
2 slices stale white bread, torn into
    large pieces
2 garlic cloves, roughly chopped
1 tablespoon sherry vinegar
2 tablespoons extra virgin olive oil

*Seafood*

• To make the romesco sauce, place the almonds, roasted capsicum, paprika, bread pieces, garlic and vinegar in the bowl of a food processor. Process until smooth, then gradually add enough of the olive oil until you have a thick sauce. Cover and refrigerate. ▶

► • Prepare the seafood. Cut the fish into 2 cm (3/4 inch) cubes. Clean the squid tubes and cut into rings. Scrub the mussels and clams with a stiff brush. Pull out the hairy beards from the mussels. Discard any broken mussels or clams or open ones that don't close when tapped on the work surface. Peel the prawns, leaving the tails intact. Gently pull out the dark vein from each prawn back, starting at the head end. Refrigerate the seafood until needed.

• Heat the oil in an 8 litre (280 fl oz) pressure cooker over medium heat and cook the leek for 5 minutes or until starting to soften. Add the red and green capsicum and cook for a further 5 minutes or until the leek is soft. Add the garlic, chilli, paprika and bay leaf and cook for 2 minutes or until aromatic. Add the wine and saffron and simmer for 2 minutes.

• Add the stock, brandy, lemon juice, tomatoes and parsley sprigs to the cooker. Season with salt and freshly ground black pepper. Bring to the boil over high heat. Lock the lid in place and bring the cooker to high pressure over high heat. Once high pressure is reached, reduce the heat to stabilise the pressure and cook for 8 minutes.

• Remove the cooker from the heat and release the pressure using the quick release method. Remove the lid carefully.

• Add the prepared seafood to the pressure cooker, replace the lid immediately and lock in place. Bring the cooker to low pressure over high heat. Once low pressure is reached, reduce the heat to stabilise the pressure and cook for a further 2 minutes.

• Remove the cooker from the heat again and release the pressure using the quick release method. Remove the lid carefully.

• Discard any mussels or clams that remain closed. Remove the parsley sprigs from the soup. Stir enough of the romesco sauce through the zarzuela to thicken it slightly. Divide among serving bowls and top with the remaining sauce. Sprinkle with the chopped parsley and serve with lemon wedges and crusty bread.

# PRAWN GUMBO

preparation time: 25 minutes
cooking time: 25 minutes
serves: 4–6

1 kg (2 lb 4 oz) raw prawns (shrimp)
1 tablespoon peanut oil
4 bacon slices, trimmed of fat, diced
1 onion, finely chopped
1 red capsicum (pepper), seeded and
   chopped
1 garlic clove, crushed
2 teaspoons dried oregano
1¹/2 teaspoons dried thyme

1 teaspoon sweet paprika
¹/4 teaspoon cayenne pepper
2 bay leaves
60 ml (2 fl oz/¹/4 cup) dry sherry
300 ml (10¹/2 fl oz) fish stock
150 ml (5 fl oz) tomato juice
100 g (3¹/2 oz/¹/2 cup) long-grain rice
150 g (5¹/2 oz) okra, sliced
1 tablespoon olive oil

• Peel the prawns, leaving the tails intact. Gently pull out the dark vein from each prawn back, starting at the head end. Cover and refrigerate until needed.

• Heat oil in a 6 litre (210 fl oz) pressure cooker over medium–high heat and cook the bacon for 5 minutes or until crisp. Remove and set aside. Reduce the heat to medium, add the onion and cook for 10 minutes or until softened. Add the capsicum, garlic, oregano, thyme, paprika, cayenne pepper and bay leaves and cook for 3 minutes or until aromatic. Add the sherry and simmer for 2 minutes, scrapping the base of the pot.

• Return the bacon to the cooker with the stock, tomato juice, rice and okra and stir well. Lock the lid in place and bring the cooker to low pressure over high heat. Once low pressure is reached, reduce the heat to stabilise the pressure and cook for 5 minutes.

• Meanwhile, heat the olive oil in a large non-stick frying pan over medium–high heat and cook the prawns in batches, if necessary, for 1 minute each side or until just cooked through. Remove from the pan and set aside.

▶

▶ • Remove the cooker from the heat and release the pressure using the natural release method. Remove the lid carefully. Stir the prawns through the gumbo and serve immediately.

# SEAFOOD FIDEOS

**preparation time:** 25 minutes
**cooking time:** 20 minutes
**serves:** 4–6

300 g (10$^{1}/_{2}$ oz) raw prawns (shrimp)
300 g (10$^{1}/_{2}$ oz) firm white fish fillets
200 g (7 oz) squid tubes
1 kg (2 lb 4 oz) mussels
125 g (4$^{1}/_{2}$ oz) fideos or vermicelli
   pasta (see Note)
1 tablespoon olive oil
1 onion, finely chopped
1 garlic clove, finely chopped

$^{1}/_{2}$ teaspoon chilli flakes
60 ml (2 fl oz/$^{1}/_{4}$ cup) seafood,
   chicken or vegetable stock
1 x 400 g (14 oz) tin chopped
   tomatoes
2 tablespoons chopped oregano
chopped flat-leaf (Italian) parsley,
   to garnish

• Prepare the seafood. Peel the prawns, leaving the heads and tails intact. Gently pull out the dark vein from each prawn back, starting at the head end. Cut the fish into 3 cm (1$^{1}/_{4}$ inch) pieces. Cut the squid tubes into 1 cm ($^{1}/_{2}$ inch) rings. Scrub the mussels with a stiff brush and pull out the hairy beards. Discard any broken mussels or open ones that don't close when tapped on the work surface.

• Break the noodles into 5 cm (2 inch) lengths. Add to a saucepan of boiling water and cook until al dente. Drain, rinse and set aside.

• Meanwhile, heat the oil in a 6 litre (210 fl oz) pressure cooker over medium heat and cook the onion for 5 minutes or until starting to soften. Add the garlic and chilli and cook for a further 1 minute or until aromatic. Add the stock, tomatoes and oregano to the cooker and bring to the boil over high heat. Stir in the prepared prawns, fish, squid rings and mussels. Lock the lid in place and bring the cooker to low pressure over high heat. Once low pressure is reached, reduce the heat to stabilise the pressure and cook for 2 minutes or until the seafood is just cooked.

• Remove the cooker from the heat and release the pressure using the quick release method.

• Divide the noodles among large serving bowls and immediately ladle the seafood and the juices over. Sprinkle with the parsley and serve with warmed flour tortillas.

*Note Fideos is a traditional Mexican or Spanish dish. The word refers to the noodle that is used, which is a very thin, vermicelli-like pasta. If you can't find fideos noodles, use vermicelli or capellini pasta.*

# SPICY FISH CURRY

**preparation time:** 15 minutes
**cooking time:** 15 minutes
**serves:** 4

1 tablespoon peanut oil
5 green chillies, seeded and chopped
2 dried red chillies, chopped
1/2 cinnamon stick
2 teaspoons grated fresh ginger
2 garlic cloves, finely chopped
4 sprigs curry leaves (optional)
1 teaspoon ground turmeric
1/4 teaspoon chilli powder
1 teaspoon curry powder

1 x 400 ml (14 fl oz) tin coconut milk
250 ml (9 fl oz/1 cup) fish or chicken
    stock
2 ripe tomatoes, finely chopped
800 g (1 lb 12 oz) snapper fillets, cut
    into 2.5 cm (1 inch) pieces
2 spring onions (scallions), sliced
    diagonally
juice of 2 limes, or to taste

▶

▶ ● Heat the oil in a 6 litre (210 fl oz) pressure cooker over medium heat and cook the green and red chilli, cinnamon stick, ginger, garlic, curry leaves (if using), turmeric, chilli powder and curry powder, stirring, for 2 minutes or until aromatic. Add the coconut milk, stock and tomato and stir well.

● Lock the lid in place and bring the cooker to high pressure over high heat. Once high pressure is reached, reduce the heat to stabilise the pressure and cook for 10 minutes.

● Remove the cooker from the heat and release the pressure using the quick release method. Remove the lid carefully.

● Stir in the fish, replace the lid immediately and lock in place. Bring the cooker to low pressure over high heat. Once low pressure is reached, reduce the heat to stabilise the pressure and cook for 2 minutes or until the fish is just cooked through.

● Remove the cooker from the heat and release the pressure using the quick release method. Remove the lid carefully.

● Stir through half the spring onion and add most of the lime juice, then taste to see if more lime juice is needed. Garnish with the remaining spring onion and serve with steamed rice.

Seafood

# JAMBALAYA

**preparation time:** 20 minutes
**cooking time:** 20 minutes
**serves:** 4

16 raw prawns (shrimp)

2 boneless, skinless chicken breasts

4 vine-ripened tomatoes

1/2 teaspoon saffron threads

2 tablespoons olive oil

3 bacon slices, rind and fat
   removed, chopped

2 chorizo sausages, cut into 1 cm
   (1/2 inch) slices diagonally

1 red onion, sliced

1 small red capsicum (pepper),
   seeded and sliced

1 small green capsicum (pepper),
   seeded and sliced

2 garlic cloves, finely chopped

1–2 teaspoons seeded and finely
   chopped jalapeño chilli

3 teaspoons Cajun spice mix

1 teaspoon smoked paprika

400 g (14 oz/2 cups) long-grain
   rice, rinsed

500 ml (17 fl oz/2 cups) chicken stock

250 ml (9 fl oz/1 cup) beer

*Seafood*

• Peel the prawns, leaving the tails intact. Gently pull out the dark vein from each prawn back, starting at the head end. Trim the chicken and cut into 1.5 cm x 6 cm (5/8 inch x 21/2 inch) strips. Cover separately and place in the refrigerator.

• Score a cross in the base of each tomato. Put the tomatoes in a heatproof bowl and cover with boiling water. Leave for 30 seconds, then transfer to cold water, drain and peel the skin away from the cross. Cut the tomatoes into quarters and set aside.

• Put the saffron in a small bowl with 1 tablespoon warm water and set aside for 10 minutes to soak.

• Meanwhile, heat half the oil in a 6 litre (210 fl oz) pressure cooker over medium–high heat and cook the bacon and chorizo for 5 minutes or until crisp. Remove and set aside. Reduce the heat to medium, add the onion and red and green capsicum  ▶

▶ to the cooker and cook for 5 minutes or until starting to soften. Add the garlic, chilli, spice mix and paprika and cook for a further 2 minutes or until aromatic.

● Add the rice to the cooker and stir to coat well in the spices. Stir in the tomato quarters, saffron mixture, stock and beer. Place the chicken on top. Lock the lid in place and bring the cooker to low pressure over high heat. Once low pressure is reached, reduce the heat to stabilise the pressure and cook for 6 minutes.

● Meanwhile, heat the remaining oil in a large non-stick frying pan over medium–high heat and cook the prawns in batches, if necessary, for 1 minute each side or until just cooked through. Remove from the pan and set aside.

● Remove the cooker from the heat and release the pressure using the quick release method. Remove the lid carefully. Stir through the prawns and serve immediately.

## BOUILLABAISSE

**preparation time:** 25 minutes
**cooking time:** 25 minutes
**serves:** 6

200 g (7 oz) firm white fish fillets,
   such as monkfish
200 g (7 oz) salmon fillet
12 mussels
12 raw prawns (shrimp)
2 tomatoes
1 tablespoon olive oil
1 leek, white part only, chopped
1 carrot, chopped
1 celery stalk, chopped
1 fennel bulb, roughly chopped

2 garlic cloves, crushed
coarsely grated zest of 1 orange
250 ml (9 fl oz/1 cup) fish stock
100 ml (3$^1$/$_2$ fl oz) dry white wine
   or pernod
pinch saffron threads
1 tablespoon tomato paste
   (concentrated purée)
chopped flat-leaf (Italian) parsley,
   to garnish

- Prepare the seafood. Cut the white fish into 2 cm (3/4 inch) pieces. Remove any bones from the salmon using your fingers or a pair of tweezers, and cut the salmon into 2 cm (3/4 inch) pieces. Scrub the mussels with a stiff brush and pull out the hairy beards. Discard any broken mussels or open ones that don't close when tapped on the work surface. Peel the prawns, leaving the tails intact, then gently pull out the dark vein from each prawn back, starting at the head end. Cover and refrigerate the seafood until needed.

- Score a cross in the base of each tomato. Put the tomatoes in a heatproof bowl and cover with boiling water. Leave for 30 seconds, then transfer to cold water, drain and peel the skin away from the cross. Cut the tomatoes in half and roughly chop the flesh.

- Heat the oil in a 6 litre (210 fl oz) pressure cooker over medium heat and cook the leek for 5 minutes or until starting to soften. Add the carrot, celery, fennel, garlic and orange zest and cook for a further 5 minutes or until aromatic.

- Stir in the tomato, stock, wine, saffron and tomato paste. Lock the lid in place and bring the cooker to high pressure over high heat. Once high pressure is reached, reduce the heat to stabilise the pressure and cook for 10 minutes.

- Remove the cooker from the heat and release the pressure using the quick release method. Remove the lid carefully.

- Allow the soup base to cool slightly, then transfer the mixture to a food processor and process until smooth. Return to the cooker and bring to the boil over high heat. Stir in the seafood, replace the lid immediately and lock in place. Bring the cooker to low pressure over high heat. Once low pressure is reached, reduce the heat to stabilise the pressure and cook for 2 minutes or until the seafood is just cooked.

- Remove the cooker from the heat and release the pressure using the quick release method. Remove the lid carefully.

- Season with salt and freshly ground black pepper. Ladle the soup into large serving bowls and garnish with parsley. Serve with crusty bread.

# INDEX

## A
adobe pork  153
African-style lamb and peanut stew  114
apricot chicken  40
arroz con pollo  57

## B
Basque chicken  49
**beans**
    beef with root vegetables and broad
        beans  94
    Boston-style baked beans with
        ham  141
    cassoulet  154
    chilli beef with capsicum, coriander and
        avocado  73
    lamb shoulder with white beans  134
    minestrone  24
    ribollita  26
    spiced lamb with green beans  133
    spicy sausage and bean casserole  146
**beef**
    beef carbonnade  85
    beef cheeks with onions, mushrooms
        and thyme  97
    beef osso bucco  90
    beef pho  65
    beef with root vegetables and broad
        beans  94
    borscht beef  67
    braised beef short ribs  78
    chilli beef with capsicum, coriander and
        avocado  73
    corned beef with cabbage and
        potatoes  86
    country beef stew  83
    Greek-style stuffed eggplant  69

Italian meatballs with tomato sauce  70
meatloaf with tomato chutney
    sauce  79
mussaman curry  99
oxtail with marmalade  100
Portuguese beef  93
Sichuan and anise beef stew  76
stifatho  88
sukiyaki soup  68
biryani, lamb  110
borscht beef  67
Boston-style baked beans with ham  141
bouillabaisse  170
bouquet garni  135
braised veal shanks  95
brown rice and barley risotto with chicken
    and pumpkin  38
butter chicken  54
butternut pumpkin soup  17

## C
cabbage rolls  139
caldo verde  31
canja  36
cassoulet  154
cauliflower and almond soup  19
**chicken**
    apricot chicken  40
    arroz con pollo  57
    Basque chicken  49
    brown rice and barley risotto with
        chicken and pumpkin  38
    butter chicken  54
    canja  36
    chicken agrodolce  43
    chicken braised with ginger and star
        anise  50

Index